Praise for:

SPARK: Journey From Success to Significance

"Azim's message of SPARK celebrates the potential within all of us regardless of our circumstances in this guide to significance in our business and personal journeys."

Harvey Mackay, author of the #1 New York Times bestseller *Swim with the Sharks without Being Eaten Alive*

"If you would love to make a significant difference on the planet, doing exactly what you truly love with more gratitude, certainty and presence while inspiring greater enthusiasm in those you serve then Spark is the book to read."

Dr. John Demartini, international bestselling author of *The Values Factor*

"Designed for our increasingly uncertain world, SPARK is a reassuring guide to discover your purpose and how to integrate it into your daily life. Armed with practical advice, every page instructs and inspires you to explore your possibilities and expand the scope of your life."

Marshall Goldsmith, New York Times #1 bestselling author of *Triggers*, *Mojo* and *What Got You Here Won't Get You There*

"All the elements Azim shares in his inspiring book are time tested, proven and indeed foundational principles that can ignite the SPARK within you and create optimum impact in the lives of others. Read this book and you'll reap the dividends. I highly recommend it!"

    Dr. Nido Qubein, president of High Point University

"Azim Jamal has much wisdom to share with the world in need of more wisdom"

    Robin Sharma, author of
    #1 worldwide bestseller *The 5 AM Club*

"This is indeed a book for everyone ... who dare to search for answers, and who are unafraid to SPARK a change in their lives. This is a must-read and I, myself, have learned these valuable lessons in my journey that I will continue to use here and beyond."

    Extract from the Foreword by Brian Tracy,
    author of #1 international bestseller *Eat That Frog*

"The shift from seeking Success to Significance is extremely difficult, but it's worth the effort. It won't only change your life, but also those in your inner circle. In this book, Azim Jamal lays out a roadmap. All you have to do is follow it."

    Nick Nanton, EMMY® Award winning director/producer

"*Azim writes with passion, wisdom and love. This book is his gift to you. Enjoy!*"

Harvey McKinnon, international
bestselling co-author of *The Power of Giving*

"*In* SPARK: Journey from Success to Significance, *Azim Jamal has masterfully assembled a bible of parables that address many of the challenges of our hectic modern lives. By following Azim's guidance I have no doubt that our lives will be enhanced and our impact will be amplified.*"

Roger Killen, founder & producer,
Get Inspired Talks

"SPARK *and the principles it teaches through the beautiful story it tells, will help you become the best version of yourself and make the greatest contribution you can in life.*"

Brian Walsh, founder & CEO,
Real Success Network

Also by Azim Jamal

CORPORATE SUFI SERIES

Books
What You Seek is Seeking You
Business, Balance & Beyond
Life Balance the Sufi Way
The Power of Giving
The One-Minute Sufi
The Corporate Sufi
Journal for Lasting Happiness
Seven Steps to Lasting Happiness

Audio CDs
Seven Steps to Lasting Happiness
The Power of Giving
Love
Power
Ignite your Untapped Potential

SPARK
Journey from Success to Significance

Azim Jamal
Foreword by BRIAN TRACY

Corporate Sufi
Business, Balance & Beyond

Published by Corporate Sufi Worldwide Inc.
3718 Oak Street, Vancouver, BC
Canada V6H 2M3
info@corporatesufi.com
www.corporatesufi.com

© Azim Jamal

Published in arrangement with
Azim Jamal
10151 Gilmore Crescent
Richmond, BC, Canada, V6X 1X1

SPARK
ISBN 978-0-2288-8596-2 (Hardcover)
ISBN 978-0-2288-8595-5 (Paperback)
ISBN 978-0-2288-8597-9 (eBook)

No part of this book may be reproduced or utilized in
any form or by any means, electronic or
mechanical including photocopying, recording or by any
information storage and retrieval system,
without permission in writing from the publishers.

Acknowledgments

I dedicate the book to all those who live with SPARK—taking the journey from Success to Significance. And to my family, Farzana, Sahar and Tawfiq, for their unconditional support and love.

Deep thanks to the following:

- Shailaja Sharma, who is part of the Corporate Sufi team. The fable in the book was contracted to her. She conceived and crafted the story and was instrumental in thinking through the intricacies required to make the story appealing to a wide audience.
- Our professional editor, Gabrielle Moss, for her insightful edits, guidance and feedback.
- Sheila Robb, for her wise and thoughtful comments.
- Team members Nerella Campigotto and Altaz Jamal for their multiple edits and invaluable feedback throughout the process of completing the book.
- Salim Dewji, Brett Fleming, Salim Premji and Mohamed Manji for their guidance.
- My daughter, Sahar Jamal, for several edits over the course of this journey; my son, Tawfiq Jamal, for his feedback; and my wife, Farzana, for her amazing support whilst I burnt the midnight oil for long periods of time over the past two years while writing this book.
- Input from many other colleagues and friends—too many to name them all. Thank you all for sharing your guidance and feedback. Much appreciate your contribution!

Foreword

Let me begin this foreword by reminding you of the immense and intense energy you all individually possess! This energy powers your intentions, your actions, your dreams and your truths and is the fuel for your ultimate success.

This book enlightens you on how to realize, internalize and optimize this valuable gift. You have led yourself here to read this book because it is timely for you and because you attract what you aspire to! Consider yourself one of the lucky ones to have heeded the call of your inner voice.

Azim, whom I have had the pleasure of getting to know through our speaking engagements and co-authorship, is a calm, composed and conscious human being. I have seen this firsthand in how he deals with and amicably dissolves any tense situation facing him. In how he rarely, if ever, allows external factors to negatively impact his internal peace. How he always appears centered and poised, no matter the circumstance. Whether he is on stage or off, whether one-on-one or in a group, Azim is authentic, congruent and highly effective.

In this book, Azim shares his secrets to achieving significance and a well-balanced but highly potent passion for pursuing your life's purpose—all by using tools you already possess.

I have written over 90 books, produced several hundred self-help programs and spoken to more than five million people around the world. My work has brought me happiness, pleasure and purpose. But, most of all, my experiences have brought me to the realization that my greatest success has come from recognizing, acknowledging and acting upon my inner SPARK. This is what Azim will convey to you in this book, and I support what he shares because I know it works. In fact, I highly recommend its use in your everyday life.

The fable—a simple but riveting tale of a successful yet unfulfilled lawyer, transformed by a journey he never wanted to take—is both inspiring and motivating. And with each brilliantly woven-in self-help section, Azim builds on the story to provide you with a practical blueprint to unleashing your SPARK

This is indeed a book for everyone, but especially for those who dare to question, who dare to search for answers, and who are unafraid to SPARK a change in their lives. This is a must-read, and I, myself, have learned these valuable lessons in my journey that I will continue to use here and beyond.

Enjoy!

Brian Tracy
#1 International Bestselling Author of *Eat That Frog*

Contents

Acknowledgments	vii
Foreword	xi
Introduction	1
PART 1	**9**
Story: Self to Selflessness	11
Significance: S for *Service*	45
PART 2	**59**
Story: Millennial Wisdom	61
Significance: P: for *Purpose*	73
PART 3	**87**
Story: Apricot Man	89
Significance: A for *Attraction*	115
PART 4	**125**
Story: Peak Performance	127
Significance: R for *Resilience*	139
PART 5	**151**
Story: A Bridge to Know Where!	153
Significance: K for *Knowing*	183
Final Thoughts	**193**

End Notes	205
Introducing... **AZIM JAMAL, Inspirational Speaker and Leadership Coach**	207
Praise for **Azim's Work**	209
Develop Your SPARK and Transform **Your Success to Significance**	213

Introduction

"What are you missing in your life?" I've put that question to successful leaders all over the world. Not surprisingly, I often hear similar answers: purpose, fulfillment, happiness, balance and the like. What I've found is that many of us resign ourselves to vigorously chasing classic ideals of success without realizing that it is, in fact, "significance" that we seek.

The truth is, no matter your age, position or status, connecting your daily functions with authentic intentions and values is imperative. Otherwise, we are simply hamsters on a wheel—covering miles and miles in distance, yet never truly moving forward towards our desired destinations. Sure, there is some physical benefit from such rooted motion. But over time, it has a negative effect on matters of the heart and mind, creating a domino effect that has ongoing ramifications for our own lives and society at large.

The subtitle of this book, "Journey from Success to Significance," was borne from my own expeditions and explorations, all of which helped me form a steadfast belief: that we are all destined, by our very nature, to be explorers—pioneers who intrinsically understand that it is the journey, and not the destination, that matters. It is the twists and turns of life that guide our principles.

What I wish for you to discover is that a life of significance is not some unattainable, pie-in-the-sky dream. Rather, it is a genuine pursuit that begins with a simple acknowledgment and appreciation of what already lies within you: Natural traits fuelled by a SPARK!

The search for significance is a universal pursuit, not limited by one's experiences or means. I have been fortunate enough to work with many leaders around the world, thinkers and innovators who have amassed amazing success. Yet these brilliant people, who I'm proud to call colleagues and friends, continue to struggle with sustaining and proliferating their SPARK. I have also been blessed with many opportunities to engage in non-profit causes and work with people living in poverty, where I have seen SPARK radiate from children born in squalor, as well as from the volunteers who serve them. This observation cemented my conviction that the SPARK you carry is not dependent on any level of outward success but comes from an inward connection with your spirit.

I have spent several decades cultivating an unrelenting SPARK in my own life and attempting to inspire it in the lives of those around me. Yet, this has not always been the case. A humanitarian trip to help refugees in South Asia gave birth to my true purpose. I share the details of my experiences on this trip in my final thoughts at the end of the book; for now, I will say that while I was there, I found and experienced a real SPARK for the very first time. I learned that we bear the responsibility to serve our kin and communities through developing a guiding purpose bigger than our individual selves, which in turn attracts goodness with unwavering resilience.

So, what makes the SPARK approach different from more traditional ideas about success? The answer is its focus on what drives us. Quests for fame, power, recognition or any other self-serving form of success are driven by the ego. But any quest powered by an authentic SPARK comes from a much deeper place, one motivated by humility, modesty and the utmost regard for others' wellbeing and prosperity, not just your own. Dr. Nido Qubein, president of High Point University, put it to me:

"Success is never enough. The people who are happy reside in the zone of significance, and significance comes from one word. That one word is 'impact.'"

Those who reside in "the zone of significance" often impact every person they meet in a meaningful way that resonates beyond the need for affluence or possessions.

This does not mean that material success doesn't matter. Indeed it does because every human being deserves an honorable quality of life. However, striving for external success alone can never drive inner happiness and fulfillment.

For me, SPARK has become an all-encompassing pledge. A pledge I consciously try and sustain, no matter what transpires in my life:

I will always appreciate what I have while I continue to aim for what I want. Where there may be sadness, I will maintain a twinkle in my eye. Where there may be negativity, I will focus on radiating positive energy. I will remain authentic and be a vessel, a conduit, an instrument of the Universe that ignites spirits and inspires others. I will do my best to make a positive impact without the need for fame or recognition. Rather, I will strive to provide selfless **Service***, have a clear* **Purpose***,* **Attract** *what I aspire to and be* **Resilient** *through it all because I will allow my inner* **Knowing** *to be my guide.*

To fulfill this pledge, I have distilled its five essential principles into every facet of my life—principles that I believe can also lead you to your chosen prosperity by igniting your inner S.P.A.R.K:

S for **Service**
The more you give of yourself in service of others, the more you tap into your genius.

P for **Purpose**
Having a clear purpose in your life, one greater than yourself, creates meaning and happiness.

A for Attraction
When you visualize and dedicate yourself to your aspirations, the universe naturally inspires you to attract successful outcomes.

R for Resilience
Cultivating resilience through positive attitudes and good habits allows you to withstand any kind of adversity.

K for Knowing
Learning about your self-worth and abilities on a deeper level allows you to be confident about your aspirations and live a life of fulfillment.

As you read on, you'll meet Steve, whose life transforms, seemingly overnight, when he is forced to leave his comfort zone to complete a task he sees as pointless. While Steve is initially unable to connect this journey to something larger and more important than his repetitive drive for success, he soon finds hope in every circumstance and encounter in his odyssey. Steve soon realizes he is not unlike many people in the world who, although disconnected from certain parts of their purpose, are at some level aware that there is a lot more to life than what is currently on offer. He soon grasps that the curveball life has thrown at him is an opportunity to transcend beyond his safe existence and engage with his desire for significance.

After every step of Steve's journey, I will highlight key messages and takeaways, offer up some reflection questions for you to ponder and propose some tips on how to get started on your own path to a life of significance. You will also have an opportunity to journal your thoughts and responses. My hope is that this will act as a practical step in helping you find and nurture your innate SPARK.

SPARK can awaken and drive you to express and manifest your innermost desire. It is the catalyst that catapults the "Present You" into the "Best You"—now and well into the future.

The SPARK you have hidden within you is yearning to come alive. All it asks of you is to recognize its existence by tapping fully into the present moment. This SPARK of possibility, though dim or dormant now, flickers within each one of us. When fuelled, it can become unshakeable!

In writing this book, I wish to inspire you to be able to ignite a fire from your SPARK, one that illuminates the path to your magnificence while also bringing light to the world.

More than ever, the world needs your glow in full flow. The time to light up your SPARK is now.

Let's get started!

PART

1

Story:
Self to Selflessness

Steve cautiously peered through his large, floor-to-ceiling windows, gazing at the carpet of lights twinkling outside his 48th-floor corner office. He immediately took a step back, feeling the same dizzying rush of blood to his face he always got when he remembered how high up he was. It was a stark reminder that his fear of heights wasn't getting any better with age.

He looked away, back towards his beautiful oak desk, which he had bought from a handmade furniture exhibition in Toronto last year. He picked a sheaf of papers up from its surface. After a year of bitter wrangling, he and Christina were finally divorced. A marriage that had begun with such aplomb a decade ago now lay in tatters (and with that 30% of his assets, too).

He flung the divorce papers down and checked his watch. It was time for his five o'clock with Michelle, his boss and CEO at Miles Inc., one of the top three management consulting firms in Canada. Steve felt a tiny rush of excitement. The COO had recently resigned to spearhead an e-commerce start-up, and the firm was looking for a replacement. There were three contenders. Steve was one of them.

His assistant, Stephanie, popped her head in to inform him she had booked an appointment with the Cypress Valley Golf Club at seven tomorrow. Cypress was an exclusive club with an invitation-only membership criterion and a whopping $50,000 in annual fees. This was more than he was paying at his existing club. The wait-list was three years long, and Steve had to nudge quite a few of his contacts to even get shortlisted for a meeting with the elite membership board that could approve or deny him entry.

Steve did not really enjoy golf. But this was the big fish pool, where the who's who of the city swam. If he wanted to be seen as a dominant player in corporate society, being seen at all the right places was very important. And no place was more right than Cypress Valley.

He adjusted his lapel and strode to the 52nd floor, another pool of big fish he was planning to make a splash with very soon.

Michelle was looking over the file for Burton—one of Steve's accounts. She looked up and motioned him inside.

"This didn't take you much time at all," she said, a smile slowly spreading over her face as she glanced at the terms.

"You know me … it never does," he chuckled, taking a seat in one of Michelle's 5,000-dollar swivel chairs.

"I thought Burton didn't want to sell."

He shrugged. "A few calls to the securities office, some deep dives into their affairs and suddenly, Burton wanted to sell and fast!"

"Looks like you also managed to get both parties just where Attenborough wanted them."

"And if you pay attention to Clause 10.3 in the addendum, we came in at 2.5% lower than what Burton was demanding," he added, adjusting his Rolex. He had to get the clasp fixed.

It was way too tight.

Michelle clapped her hands gently. "Impressive."

"That it is, and with this deal, I close this year 33% over target!"

"Not so soon …" Michelle laughed. "The deal is yet to be signed. And until it is … I am not adjusting any numbers."

"You know, Michelle, the only thing holding this back is the Burton CEO. He is out there, hiding somewhere in Barbados. He comes back on Friday, we meet on Saturday, and by the end of day on Monday, I will have this deal signed, sealed and delivered!" he said, clapping his palm on the table.

"Perfect … so, now, what about the Shapiro audit? Are your assessments in place?"

Before Steve could answer, Michelle's phone screen glowed. She glanced at it and promptly got up. "I'll have to take this one, Steve. Gimme five."

Steve nodded as she quickly walked out of the room, whispering into the phone.

Michelle never interrupted a meeting unless it was Theo Miles, the founder and chairman of the company. The man had been MIA for the last two months, which was nothing new. He disappeared for three months every year—they called it his "isolation retreat." No one except his wife and a few people at the top knew where he went. Miles claimed this gave him time to repurpose and rejuvenate.

Secretly, Steve thought it was just an excuse to get away, indulge in his secret fantasies and let off some steam. And who could blame him? After 16 years in the business, even Steve was beginning to feel jaded. Sometimes, it was difficult to just wake up and drive to work. But he knew that if he made even one small slip, somebody else would swoop in and grab everything he had worked so hard for. It was a cut-throat world, and only the powerful survived.

The door opened, and Michelle came back, looking thoughtful.

"Sorry, I'll have to cut this meeting short. It was Robert. There is an urgent review coming up, and Robert wants Theo to look at the new revisions and sign the papers. But he hasn't been able to get in touch. If Theo doesn't sign by this weekend, we could face a huge loss."

"So now what?" asked Steve.

"So, now I'll need to go and track Theo down to get the papers signed while Robert handles the client front," she sighed, simultaneously making changes in her phone calendar.

"But I wanted you to join me for the Burton deal. Can't you send someone else?" Steve said, exasperated.

Michelle pursed her lips, "I can't. But tell me if you need anything, and call when it's time to celebrate," she said, motioning her hand for a congratulatory high five. He obliged.

Steve leaned back, adjusting his hair in the reflection of her silver pen holder, "Damn sure I will. But this time, it better not be just the deal we are celebrating, right? I deserve that promotion, Mich, and you know that," he said, glancing back at her. If he didn't get the position, he could bid the Cypress Club membership goodbye. "No one has a stronger portfolio. The COO position should be mine."

Michelle smiled, "Your performance is top-notch. But the COO position is much more than that, Steve. And you know Theo … he has his own ideas."

"Come on, be honest, Mich. Theo doesn't like me much, does he? Because I don't fall in line with his charming 'save the world' ideas."

"It's not that, Steve, and you know it. Theo is the most fair and just man I know. He would never let his personal opinions interfere with what's best for the company. And his 'charming ideas,' well … those are what made him such a huge success."

Steve nodded. She wasn't wrong. The man had earned it. Eleven offices and 5,000 employees are no mean feat for someone who started out 35 years ago with one room and one client in an abandoned mill on the outskirts of Toronto. And now, even with well-established offices in London, New York and Sydney, Theo refused to move his headquarters from the mill, choosing instead to expand and develop the office space around the building rather than move location.

Sentimental, eccentric, mysterious—that's how the world saw Theo. Not a description Steve ever wanted to attribute to himself.

"Hey ... close this deal and gimme a call. I'll be with Theo then, and you can break the good news to him. And I promise I'll do my bit to push your case." Michelle smiled as she returned the Burton file.

The next day, Michelle was not in the office. Steve assumed that she had already left to meet Theo.

For a moment, he debated calling her to check, but then his own day was in full swing—three potential new client meetings, one associate lunch, a round of squash at the club, finally closing with a dinner date with the lovely Naomi, a runway model he had met at a party organized by one of his New York-based high fashion clients.

Beautiful women, fine dinners, memberships at the best clubs, a cottage in the country, a seven series BMW; he was proud to have attained the "good life"' he had always aspired to. But maintaining this "good life" had been a tiring experience. It felt like every time he managed to come close to his goal, someone would move the goalposts further away, making them more difficult to reach.

Last week, he had casually mentioned renting a house in the Hamptons for the summer to an old Harvard classmate, only to have the friend drawl back, "Ah, great, maybe I'll drop in one evening. Just bought a house there, too."

Even the Saturday brunches with his peers at the club had started to feel empty—the snide remarks, the expensive cigars, the casual cruelty, the name-dropping. They were more like peacocks strutting their stuff rather than friends catching up. It was as if nothing was intimate and honest anymore.

In the waning days of their marriage, Christina kept telling him, "You're not like the old Steve I knew. You've become so mercenary. You can't do one thing if there is nothing bigger in it for you, can you?"

He grinned at the irony of that statement. She hadn't been any less mercenary while negotiating her settlement.

So, what if she left him? There were always prettier women, faster cars, more beautiful homes to amuse him with. The new Jaguar F-Pace would go a long way to reviving the old Steve. He had his eye on that car ever since its launch three months ago, and if …

The phone rang. It was Michelle.

"Hey, Mich. Are you at the airport?"

"No. That's actually the reason I called. I was stepping out of the shower this morning, slipped and twisted my ankle. Richard is on his way home to take me to the ER. I assume they'll need to take an X-ray to rule out a fracture. Long story short—I don't see how I'll be able to travel. You'll have to go in my place. The flight from Pearson International to Delhi departs at 11:30 tonight. Call Sandra … she's already working on your tickets."

"Hey, Michelle, hold on. Sorry about your foot. But I can't go anywhere. You know … the Burton deal … on Saturday … I have to be here!" Plus, Steve had the Cypress Club meeting tomorrow, and that was as important.

"Don't worry about that; I'll tell Susan or Narayen to take over for you."

Susan and Narayen? The very people who were fiercely vying for the COO position. "Over my dead body!" screamed Steve's inner voice.

"You can't be serious, Mich. It's my deal," Steve said, trying to sound calm.

"Of course, it's your deal. And nobody can take that away from you. But what I really need you to do right now is track Theo down and get the papers signed," she pleaded. "There's nobody else who I can trust with this, Steve."

"But this is so sudden … and it's not just that I have meetings lined up for the next two days, it's—"

"Steve … Steve? Listen. It's Richard. He's home. I must go now, ok? I'm sorry to drop this one you, but you're the only one who can do it. Talk to Sandra and get the tickets." Steve heard distraction in her voice—she was still on the call, but mentally, she had moved on from the conversation.

"… And all the best on your journey!"

Click. She had hung up on him.

All the best? He couldn't believe it. Michelle was asking him to ditch the biggest meeting of his life to complete a stupid courier run and the best she could come up with was, "There's nobody else who I can trust." This was freaking ridiculous!

After the deal was signed, Steve planned to drive to the cottage with Naomi. Now all his plans were going to be shelved.

Steve paced the room, thinking of plausible excuses. Why couldn't Susan or Narayen go in his place? If they could replace him for his deal, they surely could also replace him for the Delhi jaunt.

He picked up his phone and asked Stephanie to connect

him to Narayen. A few minutes later, she called back. Narayen was on leave and not set to return for the next couple of days. He was off the grid and not reachable by phone.

Steve couldn't ask Susan to go in his place—not after the way he had snagged the Ryder account from right under her nose. But Michelle could tell her!

"Siri, call Mich!"

"Calling Mich," confirmed Siri.

But Michelle didn't answer. The call just went to voicemail.

It seemed that Steve had hit a dead end. There was no one else he could call. And he couldn't get someone else to go without getting Michelle's approval first—she had been very clear about the secrecy of those documents.

Steve poured himself a stiff drink and gulped it down. Even the full-bodied, mature oak, ginger and raisin flavors of the Macallan 18 tasted like sewage right now. He stepped out onto the balcony and thrust his face against the evening breeze, closing his eyes so he wouldn't be tempted to look down. It was only October, but there was already a delicious fall nip in the air.

He couldn't see any way around it. The plane was leaving in three hours, and he would be on it.

The first call he made was to Attenborough. He informed him that he would not be able to attend but assured him the deal would move forward as planned. Next, he called his counterpart at Burton to ensure there were not going to be any last-minute surprises in the agreement. Then, he summoned his team to strategize the meetings and depositions they would need to handle in his absence.

Finally, he called up the Cypress Club and tried to reschedule the meeting for next week. The General Manager coolly remarked that next week was not possible and briefly hinted that it would be best if Steve did not miss this meeting, especially if he was really keen on the membership.

Twenty minutes later, Stephanie quietly walked into his office with two envelopes. One was a large brown manila envelope. The other, a smaller white one, held his plane tickets.

She had already asked his driver, Charles, to pick up Steve's suits from the dry-cleaner and wait for him in the parking garage. And, if Steve left immediately, he would still have time to make a pit stop at Maison Boulud for his favorite steak dinner. Aah Stephanie! The quiet, super-efficient Stephanie, always thinking three steps ahead!

He ran down to the garage, jumped in the car, and quickly examined the package meant for Theo. It was nondescript at best, except for the seal. He switched on the car's interior light and held the envelope up against the bulb, hoping to glean some information about the contents. But no matter how many ways he tilted the envelope up to the light, here was no indication at all of the secrets it held.

Then, he turned his focus to the tickets, making sure they had booked him an aisle seat. He then glanced at the destination. Dharamsala?! Where the heck was Dharamsala?

He quickly began to Google the city. It was one thing traveling to a country he had only heard about, but another to go to a city he had never known even existed until just now.

Charles sped Steve home to grab his overnight bag, vitamins, bulletproof coffee, and passport. They were out on the road again in no time.

The ride to the airport was quiet, and Charles, sensing his boss's mood, refrained from attempting any polite conversation. Steve tried calling Michelle one more time, but again she didn't answer.

He suddenly remembered that he hadn't called Naomi to cancel their dinner plans. She had been in Milan for a show and was back in Toronto today. As he dialed her number, his mind wandered into thoughts of her. His friend Ali was right. He did have a type—tall, leggy and beautiful.

After leaving a message for Naomi, he once again Googled the city he was being dragged to. Dharamsala was a small hillside town, a holiday destination in Northern India. The only notable features of the town were its hills and that it was the current residence of the Dalai Lama, the exiled Tibetan spiritual leader.

And Theo was not even in the main town but plonked in some village *near* Dharamsala. Trust Theo to pick the most obscure places on the planet.

But Miles Inc. did have an office in New Delhi. He could stop there on his way back. And Theo would be with him … that would make this forced trip feel a little better. Come to think of it, if nothing else, this was a great opportunity to impress Theo in person.

And if he finished all this soon, he could still make it back just in time to close his deal.

Twenty hours and two flight changes later, an exhausted and sleepy Steve arrived at Indira Gandhi International Airport in Delhi. His connecting flight for Dharamsala was exactly two hours from touchdown. He cleared immigration and rushed to terminal 3D, snaking in through a thick crowd of people and piles of luggage. That's when he noticed the weather. The skies had opened, and it was pouring mercilessly.

The pretty girl with kohl-lined eyes behind the counter took one look at his tickets and shook her head sadly. "Sorry, sir, this flight has been canceled."

"Book me on the next one, then."

"That's in two days, sir … for 4:30 pm on Tuesday."

Steve was shocked.

"Two days … two freaking days! I can't wait that long!"

"I am sorry, sir; there are no daily flights," the girl replied.

"But this will ruin my schedule. There must be another way to get to this … this … Dharamsala!"

"Sir, you can take an overnight bus or cab."

"Lady, I don't do buses. But cabs … now, where can I book one?"

"Sir, you will find many options outside the airport … and sir, try to book—"

Steve had already turned and was walking away before she could even finish her sentence. He remembered that the office had arranged a cab to pick him up from the Dharamsala airport. But now, with these delays and changes, the entire schedule would have to be rearranged. He sent a message to the Delhi Corporate Travel Desk to cancel the cab and only rebook it as per his further instructions, which he would send by morning.

He grabbed a coffee from the Starbucks kiosk beside the exit but decided against the grilled sandwich. Too many carbs. It had been three months since he had started his ketogenic diet, and the results were already showing. He had dropped 25 pounds. He decided he would only eat again when he reached Dharamsala.

When he got there, Steve planned to book himself in the best five-star he could find and eat a big breakfast—eggs, chicken and a green salad, ideally something local. Then he'd shower, put on his best suit and head over to impress Theo in that godforsaken village he was hunkered in.

By the time he'd made his way out of the terminal, the rains had subsided. But the heat hit him like a wall, cloying and damp, swathing his body in sweat. And the people! So many people! The funky smells, mixed with the noise of traffic, immediately overpowered his senses. It was like entering a freaking carnival.

Steve took off his jacket and looked around. On cue, a small crowd of people surrounded him. They were all cab and tuk-tuk drivers peddling their rides. One of them spoke in English, offering to take him wherever he wanted and pointed to a white Toyota parked across the road. After a quick back and forth, the man agreed to take him to Dharamsala for just 8,000 rupees. Not a large amount, but nonetheless, Steve decided to check out the rates on Uber.

The network on his phone was still not working, so he looked for an Uber counter. He saw one, but there was a long line of people impatiently waiting as they fanned themselves. Suddenly, the driver with the clean white Toyota looked very appealing.

Steve tracked down the man with whom he made the 8,000-rupee deal, and he was quickly led to the car. Upon arriving at the car, the man handed Steve's bag to the driver and then opened the back door for Steve to take a seat. He entered the car, and the driver immediately turned on the air conditioning, blasting him with cold air that smelled like a mix of tobacco, stale food and cheap fruity perfume, making him nauseous.

While inhaling through his mouth, he asked the driver to max up the AC to full blast and keep driving straight to Dharamsala. He didn't want to stop anywhere for food, coffee, sightseeing or anything else.

After an hour of driving through city streets thick with traffic, the road gradually widened into a highway. Lulled by the constant speed and the cool air flowing through the AC vents, Steve began to doze. He tied the handles of the overnight bag around his wrist, put his phone in his inner pocket, rolled his sleeve over his Rolex, and settled back in his seat for a nap.

He didn't know how long he had been asleep when he felt something sharp poking his neck. He opened his eyes and instantly froze as he felt the sharp edge of a knife pricking his neck. It was dark, but he could see someone's outline looming over him.

The man prodded Steve's neck with the knife and muttered something in the local language. Grabbing him by his collar, the man forcefully dragged Steve out of the car.

Steve was pushing the knife-wielding man back when suddenly, someone else grabbed and twisted Steve's arm behind him. The driver was not alone. One more man suddenly leaped out from behind a tree, nervously gripping a small revolver with both hands. He kept licking his lips, his gaze constantly darting at the others as if asking for backup.

Steve tried to present a calm demeanor as he gulped down the bitter rush of bile that rose in his throat. His heartbeat was rapid, and sweat quickly formed on his palms and armpits. He thought back to all the crime TV shows he used to watch. On all of them, appearing calm in the face of danger was shown to be an asset—the thing that kept a scary situation from getting worse. But Steve didn't know if he appeared calm. He was sure his heart was beating so fast, even the men robbing him could hear it.

He scanned his surroundings. They were standing on a small dirt road that ran alongside a large field planted with tall grass of some kind. Except for the sound of a dog howling and wind rustling through the blades of grass, the night was silent. There were no lights, no houses, no places to run to or people who could stop this.

So, this was how he was going to die? Shot by a few punks

on a dirt road in the middle of nowhere? Was this what his life was worth? A couple of hundred dollars?

Using broken English, the driver threatened Steve, telling him to keep quiet. He motioned Steve to hand over everything in his pockets while the second man held him by his shoulders. Steve must have been taking too long for his liking, for the driver suddenly grabbed for Steve's pockets himself, digging out his wallet and iPhone. Holding Steve's arm still, the driver unclasped the Rolex from his wrist.

Steve tried to say something but was immediately sent reeling by a blow to his face.

A humming noise reverberated in his head and, for a moment, everything went dark. When he came to, Steve was sprawled on the road. He felt something wet trickling down his nose and reached up to touch it. It was blood.

The bandits had unzipped his overnight bag and flung it upside down, emptying the contents onto the road. His clothes, wads of Indian and Canadian currency, reading glasses, three protein bars, and the manila envelope all laid bare for the taking.

The third man pulled out a large scarf from his pocket and started piling everything into it. Ordering Steve to stay down, two of the robbers ran back to the car while the man with the revolver stood guard over him.

"Hey, at least leave the phone," Steve pleaded. "How will I go on otherwise?"

"You thank your god … we not murder you," the man with the revolver hissed.

"But the phone … My whole life is on that phone. Please … I don't know anyone here."

The man with the revolver glared at Steve. "You think we fools … we go, and you call police … on phone?"

"OK, fine," Steve said, trying to collect himself. He tried

to pretend to himself that this was just another deal—just a deal he had to negotiate.

"Please," he implored the man with the revolver. "Please just leave me the damn envelope. The brown packet ... please. It's of no value to you, but if I lose it, I will lose my job. Please."

The gunman shouted something at the other two. Then, the driver removed the envelope and shook it to make sure it did not have any cash. Satisfied that it was worthless, he flung it in Steve's direction. The gunman then bolted to the car, and the three men drove off, splattering Steve's clothes with muddy water.

Steve picked up the fallen envelope and slipped it inside his shirt. He brushed the mud off his clothes, discovering that his pocket had been ripped off in the struggle. He lifted one leg out of his Armani loafers, which were now squishy with rainwater, to make sure that his foot hadn't been injured, that he could still walk. As he went to check the time, he was painfully reminded they had taken the Rolex, as well.

The moon began to peek out from a pool of clouds, flooding the field in a wash of silver, illuminating the only possession he had left—the manila envelope.

Steve started walking, shuddering every time his expensive loafers squished in the rain puddles. After an hour of walking aimlessly down a desolate road, with no phone, no directions and just the sound of wind rustling through the field for company, he could, for the first time in a long time, hear his own thoughts. Unsurprisingly, they were not optimistic.

Why me? Why here? Why now? What now? How long can I keep on walking? What if those men come back and shoot me? Would I die in this godforsaken dump alone? Seven thousand miles away from home. Nobody even knows me here. If I died back home, at least the Toronto Star *would have carried my obituary. Mother would have hosted a quiet but beautiful funeral. People from the office would have attended. My golf buddies. Naomi.*

Here, he would most probably be cremated, consigned to flames, with no one to honor him as he became dust in a foreign land.

He did not deserve this. But did anyone deserve this? This complete and utter annihilation?

Steve turned the thought over in his mind.

Serial killers and pedophiles?

But then, there were many innocent people who suffered. Yesterday, he had read about a four-year-old who had fallen under the wheel of his school bus while getting off it. And Kobe Bryant, his favorite athlete, had been killed in a freak helicopter accident. Bad things happen, he thought—sometimes to the best of people.

Where was the meaning in all of this, then? Was life just an endless series of meaningless events? It felt strange how this had never occurred to him before. Until now, his comfortable life made him oblivious to such questions. His cozy existence made it easy for everything to be about the next goal, the next promotion, the next … something. It was as if he was living his life always leaning into the future while never fully consuming the present.

The pastor at his mother's church said that life by itself had no meaning. It was in our hands to create meaning. Was that true?

It had taken a whole new continent and a near-death experience to force him to even think about this stuff.

So, could he create meaning, even in all of this? His mother was the best example. Widowed at 32, she had worked two jobs, denying herself comforts to put her three children through college. And still, she managed to emerge happy and hopeful. She said that even when things were the darkest, life always gave her enough to get by and find something to feel grateful for. And he had to admit, now in her seventies, living in a tiny one-bedroom apartment, she was still happy with life.

As he trudged along, Steve tried to think about the situation the way his mother would. There was a silver lining. Things could have gone much worse. Those men could have killed him or pushed him out of the running car. At least he had his life.

But what kind of life was this, exactly? What meaning had he infused it with or even extracted from it? Was it merely one that confined him to producing big wins for his clients and collecting a few fancy possessions along the way? If he had gotten killed back there, how many people would truly miss him?

He increased his speed, with thoughts raging inside of him like the storm-filled skies above him. But slowly, as the minutes ticked by, a different kind of light embraced him. He looked up to see the purple horizon breaking out into a swathe of fiery pink. Dawn was just breaking, and, in the illuminating light, he finally spotted the highway. It was just across the field. All this while, he had been walking alongside it.

He took off his shoes and jogged on the narrow embankment running through the field. After about 20 minutes, he heard another vehicle—a loud rattling, jangling noise. He put on his shoes and ran to the middle of the road, waving his hands. An old state transport bus came into view, its front fender dented in and the muddy white paint scraped off in several places revealing the metallic body. But to Steve, it looked as perfect as a state-of-the-art Boeing aircraft.

The driver pushed the door open, and Steve jumped

in. Every spot was taken, so the bus conductor got up and offered his seat to Steve, a narrow bench nailed to one side of the driver's compartment.

He found out that the bus was headed to Amritsar—more specifically, to some holy place, because the conductor kept folding his hands and looking up at the skies. When Steve repeated Dharamsala, the conductor seemed to understand, for he nodded and told him to buy a bus ticket once they got to Amritsar.

Hearing that there was yet another stop he would have to endure, Steve felt a familiar pull to try to get his way—to divert the damn bus and steer it straight to Dharamsala, promising him riches upon arrival that only a foreigner like him could afford.

But then, he remembered that he had no money, let alone any means of contacting Michelle to wire him cash to help him through this predicament. And the sight of a bus full of strange, tan-skinned men … one such interlude had been enough. What if this bunch also decided to kidnap him and ask for a ransom?

He decided that it was best not to draw any more attention to himself. For the first time, remaining nondescript, even invisible, seemed like a good idea.

Steve's mind then went back to the money. What would he do about the money?! Where would he come up with the ticket fare to Dharamsala? He didn't even have the money to pay for this ride. He tried to explain his predicament to the conductor and driver, but they just looked back at him blankly. They didn't understand a word he uttered. Steve slumped back in his seat, despondent.

Finally, a passenger piped up from behind. He said he spoke English and then started to express a stream of words, many of which sounded like English.

Steve explained his situation, and the man muttered something to the driver. The driver stared at him, then nodded with a smile and continued driving.

"What is he saying?" Steve asked. "You told him that I don't have money, right? Everything was stolen!"

"Yes ... Yes ... Saabji Sir ... don't worry, Saab ... he says this bus is going to God's temple. If God wants you to visit his temple, who is he to stop you? Don't worry, no money from you."

The only thing Steve could decipher was that he would not have to pay any money. And that was enough. He was already too exhausted from trying to hold on to the little handle on the side of the seat as the bus plodded, bumped and rattled through the potholes and speed breakers. He wondered why they had bothered constructing speed bumps when the potholes were already doing the job so well. Every time the bus shuddered over a pothole, a river of jarring pain shot up through Steve's nose, straight into his head. Only two hours into this long, bumpy ride and Steve had a raging headache.

Just then, the bus veered sharply, nearly throwing him off his seat. As he struggled to recover his balance, his hand flew to his chest, and he felt the outline of the envelope, the root of all his misery. Who carried envelopes anymore? He wanted to tear the damn thing apart and shred its contents to bits.

But as he held it, he had another idea. Why didn't he open it? See what exactly it was that he had risked his life for? Why wasn't he allowed to see it? Why was he supposed to travel halfway across the world without even knowing what he was carrying? What was he, a freaking carrier pigeon?

He balanced the envelope on his lap, considering. Yes, ripping it open would give him some immediate satisfaction. But what would he do after that? Hand over a ripped-open mess to an upset, disappointed Theo? He couldn't change what had already happened. But if he showed Theo how far he'd go to stick to his word and carry out his duties, maybe he'd make a good impression and get the promotion. This wouldn't all have been for nothing. He tucked the envelope back into his jacket pocket.

A whole volley of thoughts came thundering down. Though really, they were more complaints than thoughts. His brain unleashed pessimistic protests about how one stupid envelope had disrupted his perfectly manicured life and unleashed a chain of miserable events. So much for the "moment of wisdom" he had encountered on his walk, he thought. That "wisdom" had only bubbled into his brain because he was hungry and tired.

As he peered out of the window, the rain began again. Pelting against the window and thundering on the roof, it seeped in through the crevices and spaces between the glass windows, drenching him in even more misery.

Watching Steve rub his temples, a turbaned man sitting in front of him extended a strip of tablets. It was an analgesic from Pfizer. A name brand he was familiar with—OK, that was a good start. But the most important question still lingered—were they still safe and effective? A quick peek at the packaging revealed the expiry date was not for another six months.

Steve thanked the man and wondered if he'd be able to get them down without any water. A teenage boy who couldn't have been older than 14 years sat next to the man. He extended his water bottle to Steve. The choice: a splitting headache now or a potential bout of Delhi belly later. He gulped the pill with two large swallows and thanked the two.

"Mention not ... I, Balwant Singh," the man grinned, his teeth gleaming white in the low light. "My son Sukhbir," he added, pointing to the young boy by his side, who smiled shyly.

"Hello … I'm Steve Harmon."

In his mid-50s, dressed in a blue kurta and turban, with a long beard flecked with grey, Balwant Singh had piercing dark eyes and a heavy brow that constantly flickered with emotions. With just a quick glance, one could tell that he was one of those people given to great curiosity and capacity for conversation.

He worked in the State Electricity Department, he told Steve, and lived with his family in New Delhi. Today, they were on a day trip to the Golden Temple. In fact, most of the people on the bus were going to the Golden Temple. Noticing Steve's blank look at the name, Balwant explained that Harmandir Sahib, also known as the Golden Temple, was the holiest shrine for Sikhs, with millions visiting the temple each year.

Having offered details about himself, Balwant Singh now eagerly smiled at Steve, waiting for his story.

When he realized Steve was from Canada, Balwant's face lit up. In fact, many faces on the bus suddenly came alive. Steve realized a lot of Indians, especially from this part of India, had immigrated to Canada. Balwant's own nephew was employed at an IT company in Toronto.

They had a slew of questions about the country—what kind of farming did Canada have? How long did it snow? Was it true that in certain parts of the country, the sun never came out for six months? Was it easy to find Indian food? How could you get citizenship?

Suddenly, Steve found himself plunked in the role of an unofficial spokesperson for his home country, with an increasing number of passengers rapturously taking everything in, even though some didn't appear to understand a word he spoke. Soon he was being addressed as Harmaanji, though he had tried to tell them it was "Harmon," not "Harmaan."

When they heard about the mugging, an uneasy silence fell across the bus. But it was short-lived. Soon, there were offers of food, blankets and shawls, as well as suggestions about what Steve should do next. Some even went as far as inviting him to stay at their homes.

One passenger suggested that Steve talk to his uncle, who was employed with the police and could help him catch the thieves. Someone else invited him to the back, where there was more room for Steve to sit. It was as if the people on the bus had adopted him.

Steve was overwhelmed with the attention and very exhausted.

It was Sukhbir who first noticed Steve's fatigue.

"Harmanji, why don't you rest for some time. We will wake you once we reach Amritsar."

Steve accepted the offer with relief and drifted off to sleep, this time relaxed, for there was nothing more to lose.

As he dozed off, Steve started to dream of his co-worker Susan flying a plane. The wing dipping sharply on his right, ducking her craft under him and then using a thermal to soar above him effortlessly. In the dream, he too was a pilot; he switched from autopilot to manual on his fancy navigation system and wrenched the throttle back to race ahead when an air raid siren pierced the air. Ignoring the siren, he sped up his approach to get closer to the airplane ahead.

But amidst the drone of aircraft, someone kept disturbing him ... repeatedly tapping his shoulder and mumbling something.

At that instant, the siren rang out again, and Steve opened his eyes to see Balwant hovering over him. Instead of the gleaming navigation system, the bus's broken dashboard—

pasted shut with red insulating tape and decorated with shiny movie posters and a garland of multi-colored plastic flowers—plunged him back from the skies to grounded reality.

"Harmaanji. We have reached Amritsar!" Balwant exclaimed as the bus honked loudly. Steve worked to regain his senses quickly. He soon connected the dots and realized what the siren he heard had been.

However, it took Steve a moment to remember what he was doing on the bus. He glanced outside and noticed they were in the middle of a station crammed with buses and luggage. Everywhere he looked, there were people in brightly-colored clothes, wailing children, diesel fumes, and hawkers peddling their carts heaped with roasted peanuts, fried savories and fresh flowers plonked alongside a heap of used plastic water bottles, cow dung and spilled food. A big, brown Jersey cow was seated right in the middle of all of it, silently chewing her cud.

Steve disembarked from the bus, petrified, as India engulfed him with all her sensory exuberance. He quickly and nervously tapped around the front of his shirt and was relieved to feel the outline of the infamous envelope.

"Where will you go, Harmaanji? What is your plan now?" Balwant asked as he politely bowed towards Steve with respect. Balwant Singh, Steve realized, was quite a tall man. A flurry of passengers now curiously flanked the visitor from another land, all waiting for his response.

"First, I must make an urgent international call. Then, I'd really like to check into a hotel where I can have a quick wash." It had been more than 30 hours since Steve had taken a shower, and his clothes reeked of sweat, diesel and some pungent odors he was sure he had picked up entirely during his short time in India.

His throat felt scratchy. And although his headache had

subsided, there was now a dull ache behind his eyes that caused him the most irritation. He would have done anything for a hot cup of coffee. But the reality was, even if there was a coffee shop right in front of him, he didn't have any money. It was a very difficult prospect to get used to, having no money.

"I would have lent you my phone, but I don't have international calling. So, we'll go to the phone booth first," said Balwant as he led them out of the bus station.

Steve was taken aback using the word "we." He pondered how instinctually and effortlessly a stranger had enmeshed himself into his life—a prospect that both charmed and alarmed him.

Seeing Balwant take Steve under his wing, the rest of the passengers peacefully departed, though not before wishing Steve the best for his journey onward.

"Then," Balwant added, "we look for the police station to register a complaint of the missing passport." He led Steve towards a small grocery store with a telephone booth situated outside. Upon their arrival, Sukhbir began chatting with the shopkeeper.

Steve asked the shopkeeper about the call charges, but the man waved him away with a smile.

"Don't worry about the charges, Harmaanji," Balwant happily declared. "He will not take any money from you."

"Why?"

"After the painful day you just had in our country, nobody here will ask you for money," Balwant replied.

"But how does he know what my day has been like?" asked Steve.

"Call it … what is the word … intuition? He can feel your pain," explained Balwant. "Plus, I think Sukhbir may have informed him of your situation," he said with a slight laugh.

Smiling, the shopkeeper offered Steve a paper bag. It

contained a bottle of water, sanitizer and a packet of cookies.

"But it's not his fault I was robbed. Please let him know, I will pay him back once I receive some funds from my bank. I don't want him to lose out on the earnings because of me."

"He has been more than happy to help you in your time of need," Balwant explained gently. "He is also a firm believer in Karma."

Steve rolled his eyes. "Really? And what is that?"

"My peace of mind, sir. How will I sleep at night, knowing I refused someone who had just lost everything?" the shopkeeper replied.

"But this is your business. This is how you make money."

"My father always said, the more you give, the more you attract."

Steve, taken aback by the shopkeeper's staunch belief, could only shake his head with a smile.

"When you come to Amritsar next time, sir, or you write on Facebook about India, I am sure you will mention Jaimal Singh Stores," the man grinned, pointing to the signboard plastered above the entryway.

"That I will, my friend," Steve laughed.

But the shopkeeper's kindness left Steve reflecting on how he gave. He rarely, if ever, gave away something of value unless he was sure to receive something in return. Even the money he gave to charity increased his tax refund, provided some publicity or, at the very least, offered a possibility to build his network.

Despite that "give to receive" approach, he often felt he was giving so much but never receiving much in return.

But balancing the scales when giving, he realized, was never going to work. It is impossible to witness everything you receive from every act of goodness. And how could you put a price on kindness? On the generosity of spirit? On the sheer joy of helping someone.

In fact, he had been more giving when he had nothing. When he graduated from law school, his mother requested that he help a local church parishioner with a legal issue. He not only helped the man but did so without expecting any fees in return. He knew he could have refused his mother's request by claiming he was too busy, and his poor mother would have never complained. But he hadn't minded helping out. And a year later, when the parishioner invited him to a Sunday service and introduced him to the church community, Steve ended up acquiring the account of the largest local dairy in town. Until now, he had never connected the two incidents.

Steve's gaze turned to the tiny shop, with its neatly lined rows of cookie packets, chips, bottled water, juice boxes, keychains and sweets. To the shopkeeper, who was dressed in a polyester shirt that was frayed at the collar, and Balwant Singh, with his old-fashioned phone and his beaming smile. He made more in a month than these people made in a year. But today, the coin had flipped. They were more fortunate than he was because they were able to help him.

Steve entered the booth to call Michelle. Trying to stay cool and not sound frazzled, he calmly explained his situation. Michelle, stunned, immediately sprang into action—she'd organize funds and get the company's international affairs lawyer to dialogue with the Canadian embassy in India and have a new passport issued as soon as possible. But the truth was, no matter how focused Michelle was, all of this would take some time. After asking her to send all pertinent details to the shopkeeper's WhatsApp number, Steve, Balwant and the young boy made their way to the police station.

Steve registered the theft complaint with the police and was given a copy of the first information report as proof so the bank could issue new credit cards.

Steve wondered how he was going to spend the time until his next bus ride when Balwant suggested he join them at the temple.

Steve hesitated, unsure of how to explain his reluctance. "I am not religious, actually," he finally mustered the courage to say, hoping he would not offend his new friends.

Balwant shrugged. "You don't need to be religious. Being respectful is enough."

"And in the afternoon, the temple serves great food at the community Langar—all of it free, no charge!" the son added happily. "And plus, you see Indian culture!"

Ordinarily, he would not entertain such an offer in the slightest. Whenever Steve traveled abroad in the past, he had his visits planned to a T, the entire itinerary efficiently organized by a high-end travel agency that would ensure he sampled the best that any destination had to offer in the shortest amount of time possible.

But today, life was his travel service, and it had other plans. Besides, the idea of a free meal was most appealing. He didn't want Balwant to spend any more of his hard-earned money on his behalf. He also knew by now that if he refused, the father-son duo would insist on waiting there with him. And he did not want to keep them away from their schedule any further.

So, they joined the throng of people drifting to the temple. Soon, the busy market street gave way to a wide, cobbled road flanked with beautiful red buildings on either side. The buildings housed restaurants and shops selling colorful flower garlands, incense, bright scarves and books. There was even a McDonald's and a Subway.

As they walked along, the air began to hum with gentle strains of chanting. Balwant informed Steve that it was the Gurbani—the hymns of the sacred text of the Sikhs, the Guru Granth Sahib.

Steve saw that both men and women covered their heads before entering the temple. Balwant purchased a red scarf for Steve outside the temple premises and proceeded to cover his head, neatly tucking the corners behind his ears. Then, he did the same with his son, which brought a smile to Steve's face.

As soon as they stepped into the white marble-lined building, Steve saw a shoe station stacked with benches for people to sit down on to remove their shoes. Alongside it was a long row of washbasins.

A bearded man with deep-set almond eyes and a gracious smile offered to take Steve's shoes. Steve looked around. There were hundreds of pairs of shoes lying stacked in pigeon-holed silos. Then, he looked down. His tan brown, grained, calf leather shoes, rimmed with nautical-inspired rope laces, were now soggy and caked with mud. What if they misplaced his shoes or the token that identified them? What if they happened to hand them to someone else? His mind whirled with worries about his shoes, one of the only remnants of a life he had left behind in Canada.

The man patiently waited for Steve to make up his mind as a long queue of people grew behind him.

Steve released a deep sigh and finally relinquished his shoes. Walking away, he stole a long, backward glance at the column where his footwear remained. The shoe attendant's eyes met his as the man gave him a comforting nod.

Suddenly, he felt liquid beneath his feet. He looked down to see a channel recessed in the marble and filled with a continuous stream of cool water. Everyone stepped in to clean their feet before descending onto the red-carpeted floor ahead.

After a quick wash at the basin, Steve stepped into a long-arched corridor leading to the inner building. The passage opened onto a flight of stairs running down into a large marble courtyard. With each step he descended, he was taken aback by the vision of a large pool of water shimmering in ripples of gold. A sign identifying the pool as Amrit Sarover (Sacred Pool) sat next to it. Steve looked up. It was the reflection of a temple, bathed in gold, standing majestically before him.

No doubt about it—this was the famous Golden Temple he had heard Balwant talking about!

The temple rose from the middle of a grand pool as if floating in the water. The stunning edifice, flanked by a white marble courtyard and marble buildings on all sides, was constructed with marble and copper and covered with gold foil—a beautiful amalgamation of Indo-Islamic architecture. A single bridge led across the pool to the temple sanctum, which, Balwant explained, symbolized that the end goal was one for everyone.

Balwant continued to share his wisdom with Steve by asking him to notice how the temple sat lower than its surrounding buildings. Its position epitomized humility and the need to efface one's ego before entering the inner sanctum. He also pointed out the four entrances, which symbolized how everyone was welcome, irrespective of their gender, caste, religion or ethnicity.

Despite the massive crowd of people milling about, the mood was one of reflection and calm. Hymns reverberated in the courtyard as two large screens mounted on the walls showed the English translation. Children darted across the courtyard, laughing, while their families sat in groups talking softly. Some sat alone in silence, with their eyes closed, while others walked around the pathways, making their way to the temple sanctum.

Steve drifted casually along the walkway a couple of

times, enjoying the touch of the cool marble beneath his feet and soaking in the atmosphere. When Balwant and Sukhbir went inside the inner sanctum to receive the blessings, Steve sat on the steps by the pool, feet dangling in the water. Fish floated up to his feet, nibbling gently at his toes. A man with a large broom quietly mopped the floors while another wiped the railings. A young, bare-chested man took a dip in the water with folded hands. At some distance, a woman with her daughter by her side also sat by the steps, cupping the water and lifting it to her forehead as she whispered something—a prayer, perhaps. Her daughter watched with rapt attention and attempted to copy her every action.

For a moment, Steve was transported back to his childhood, to his mother's kitchen on a quiet Sunday afternoon. As he sat on the stoop near the kitchen door finishing his homework, he watched her shell peas on the counter near the window. She sang along with the radio, belting out a Carpenters' tune. The air was fragrant with the aroma of the vegetable stew simmering on the stove. He had not felt that peace for a long time.

His reverie was interrupted by someone gently tapping his shoulder. It was Sukhbir, asking him to join them for lunch at the Langar, the community kitchen.

Volunteers politely greeted each person as they entered, handing them a steel food tray, cutlery and a cup. They walked into an enormous hall lined with rows of mats on the floor. The meal was served by volunteers who scoured the halls, equipped with ladles and buckets filled with food. Everyone, irrespective of their station in life, sat together, enjoying a hearty vegetarian meal of lentils, rice, roti and yogurt.

The food was hot, fresh and fragrant, and Steve was ravenous. He devoured two helpings before remembering he had broken every cardinal rule of his ketogenic diet. But, for once, he didn't care … at all!

On their way out, Steve learned that all the work—including handling the shoe station, cleaning the courtyards, cooking the meals, rolling the countless chapatis, serving the food and cleaning the utensils—was done by volunteers. Anybody could volunteer at the temple, and many came every week. The task was enormous, considering the temple kitchen served 50,000 people on average each day, with the number going up to 100,000 people during religious occasions.

Mesmerized by how the volunteers approached their tasks, Steve had to ask. "Do they receive a commendation letter or certificate for volunteering?"

"No. There is no need for that," Balwant answered, pointing to the skies. "The universe is watching."

It was amazing to see so many people of all ages and backgrounds working together, motivated solely by a pure desire to serve.

At the shoe station, Steve returned the token and the man with the blue turban brought out his shoes and placed them on the counter.

"My shoes!" Steve gasped. They looked gleaming new. The smell of polish still lingered over them.

The man grinned, and Steve's eyes welled up. It was as if the simple joy of receiving clean shoes had somehow restored a part of him. Steve thanked him profusely and immediately felt his pocket for his wallet, eager to repay the act. He realized, yet again, that it wasn't there.

The man folded his hands and shook his head like a disappointed father looking at a child who had innocently raided the cookie jar.

Balwant Singh gently nudged Steve back from the counter.

"I wish I could give him something … something to thank

him for this."

"But you have," Balwant answered. "The opportunity to serve you. And that look in your eyes when you saw your shoes was the biggest gift of all."

Steve remembered the time, long ago, when he used to coach his local soccer team. One of the boys suffered from mild cerebral palsy and had poor motor skills. But the boy was eager to learn, and Steve had worked hard with him. The day that boy scored his first goal—the look of triumph in the boy's eyes and his mother's joyous sobbing in the stands—nothing could match that moment. He realized what Balwant said was true, even if he had forgotten it. Giving happiness to others brings you joy.

Shaken, Steve slowly followed the father-son duo back to the shopkeeper. There had been no messages from Michelle so far. Steve knew that Balwant and Sukhbir had an evening bus back to Delhi, so he urged them to carry on while he waited for the call.

After dropping Steve at the McDonalds outlet, Balwant quietly slipped a 500-rupee note into Steve's pocket.

"Mr. Singh, you and everyone here have already given me so much. I really cannot accept more."

"Please accept it, Mr. Haarmanji. You need to have some money handy for the rest of your day."

"Thanks, but …" Steve trailed off, overwhelmed and unable to meet Balwant's eyes. "I guess it's just … I have never taken so many handouts before … and all in one day. I don't know how I will ever pay this back."

"A little help is all it is—to someone who needs it right now, to feel OK about the world again, to be able to trust someone again. And if God wills it, we will meet again someday. In Delhi, or even in Canada. And then you can treat me to a good coffee there."

"What if we don't meet?"

"Then you can treat another lost traveler, and I will know it here," said Balwant pointing to his heart. "And then, we will have met again."

Significance:
S for *Service*

Even
After
All this time
The Sun never says to the Earth,
"You owe me."
Look
What happens
With a love like that,
It lights the whole sky.

—Hafiz

In this chapter, Steve is amazed at the joy and energy he sees in everyone who helps him. Their subconscious desire to attend to others fills them with unbridled delight.

What Steve witnessed is the transformative power of Service. Approaching life with a noble intention to serve others can be a powerful force—one that transforms your life from practical to phenomenal. Therefore, it is the first step to igniting your SPARK.

Let's explore some other tenets and takeaways around the concept of Service:

Look no further than nature for steadfast examples of unconditional Service.

Khalil Gibran, the Lebanese-American writer and poet, famously wrote, "It is the pleasure of the bee to gather honey from the flower and also the pleasure of the flower to yield its honey to the bee."

Nature is a great teacher of organic cycles of giving and receiving. If you have ever spent time near the mountains, watched a spectacular sunrise or sunset, witnessed the elegance of a bird in flight, or even smelled the fragrance of a flower in full bloom, you have experienced the giving-and-receiving natural order of the Earth. Much like the flower and bee, we as humans are part of nature and, in the same way, hardwired to serve. Whether we give of our time, money, knowledge or guidance, we have an innate ability and desire to support others with our resources.

A flower acts as a symbol of beauty, elegance and openness. A flower gives of its beautiful fragrance to every passerby, asking for nothing in return. It does not keep score. The same can be said about the beauty of the mountains and valleys, the glow of the sunrise and sunset, the dazzle of rainbows and everything else nature has to offer. Nature extends its bounty without expectation of return but as a pure extension of everything streaming within it.

When a cow stops giving its milk, it cannot receive more milk. When a tree bears fruit and there are no takers, the fruit eventually falls from the tree to rot. When a river stops flowing, it becomes stagnant and dies.

Nature gives unconditionally. It demonstrates abundance, humility, simplicity and grace at its finest. Nature functions with an unbound faith in Divine Timing and Universal Accounting, respecting the pure regenerative principle—the more we give, the more we create.

Your brain is hardwired for Service.

There is growing evidence that the human brain is wired for generosity. Several studies have found evidence that when people help others, their brains show activity in fundamental neural circuits, such as those that underlie parental caregiving.[1]

A wide range of research has linked different forms of generosity to better health, even among the sick and elderly. In his book *Why Good Things Happen to Good People*, Stephen Post, a professor of preventive medicine at Stony Brook University, reports that giving to others has been shown to have health benefits for people with chronic illnesses, including HIV and multiple sclerosis.

This idea of altruism behaving like a miracle drug has been around for at least two decades. The euphoric feeling we experience when we help others is what researchers call the "helper's high," a term first introduced by volunteerism and wellness expert Allan Luks to explain the powerful physical sensation associated with helping others.[2]

---

[1] Swain, James E., Sara Konrath, Stephanie L. Brown, Eric D. Finegood, Leyla B. Akce, Carolyn J. Dayton, and S. Shaun Ho. "Parenting and beyond: Common Neurocircuits Underlying Parental and Altruistic Caregiving." Parenting 12, no. 2-3 (2012): 115–23. https://doi.org/10.1080/15295192.2012.680409.

[2] Santi, Jenny. "The Science behind the Power of Giving (Op-Ed)." LiveScience. Purch, December 1, 2015. https://www.livescience.com/52936-need-to-give-boosted-by-brain-science-and-evolution.html.

Service is an opportunity, not an obligation.

Service is one of the most potent forces in the universe. The more you serve, the more you generate, create and innovate. The more you serve, the more you can tap into your genius and potential. When you embrace this principle, you invite abundance into your life. The opportunity to serve is a blessing, not a burden.

Instead of thinking about the time or money you may give up while serving, think instead of what you could gain from this gracious act. When you serve by giving money or resources, you are contributing to the forces of good karma. When you serve by giving your time, you are boosting your leadership and interpersonal skills. Any cause you freely dedicate your time and effort to is a great indication of your passion for positive change and progress.

And the skills you learn in voluntary work, like time management, patience and tenacity, are hard to learn elsewhere. When leading other volunteers, you are not motivating a team with the promise of money but by inspiring them with a cause, a purpose. This requires a different—and more powerful—skill set. It offers a chance to tap into your potential, to discover work that you are passionate about and an opportunity to build intangible leadership skills.

Most importantly, it is proof that you are someone who truly cares about contributing to the greater good, not because it is a mandated task or obligation but because you truly have a desire to help.

Therefore, treat every receiver with utmost respect, dignity and reverence. Take the approach that the Scottish philosopher William Barclay shares, "Give without remembering and receive without forgetting." Or, as Mother Teresa would say, "Do not forget to thank the people who allow you to serve them."

Service is contagious.

When we give, we are not only serving the immediate recipient of our gift; we also create a ripple effect of generosity through our community.

A study by James Fowler of the University of California, San Diego, and Nicholas Christakis of Harvard, published in the Proceedings of the National Academy of Science, shows that when one person behaves generously, it inspires other observers to behave generously later, in completely unrelated situations.[3]

In fact, the researchers found that altruism could spread by three degrees of separation. "As a result," they write, "each person in a network can influence dozens or even hundreds of people, some of whom he or she does not know and has not met."

For instance, have you ever noticed a young person helping a senior walk across a crowded road? The next time you do, pay attention to how everyone involved in the act—the young person, the senior, and even you, the observer—is impacted. The senior receives help and care, the young person receives the joy of giving and you receive a reminder of the generosity of human beings, which will lead you to act more generously yourself. That small act of kindness naturally creates a ripple effect of positivity and joy!

Ralph Waldo Emerson aptly said, "It is one of the beautiful compensations of life that no man can sincerely try to help another without helping himself." Emerson is again highlighting the universal law—the more you give, the more you create.

---

[3] Suttie, Jill Suttie Jill, and Jason Marsh Jason Marsh is the editor in chief of Greater Good. "5 Ways Giving Is Good for You." Greater Good, n.d. https://greatergood.berkeley.edu/article/item/5_ways_giving_is_good_for_you

When you give to others, you are giving to yourself. As you sow, so shall you reap. So, keep the flow of giving going!

You don't have to be rich to give.

Wealth is not defined by how much you amass, but by how much you contribute.

While on my way to do some volunteer work in the city of Khorog, Tajikistan, I had to fly through Dushanbe. From there, I was a helicopter trip away from my destination. However, due to the dense fog, I was forced to travel there by road. What was supposed to be a 12-hour ride then became a 19-hour expedition because we had four flat tires along the way. The fourth puncture occurred at 3 a.m.! As expected, it was pitch dark. The driver had little choice but to knock on a stranger's door and ask if he could borrow some light to work on the flat. We needed to be in Khorog by 8 a.m., so there was little time to waste.

To my surprise, everyone in the house sprung up to help us! A few leaped into action to prepare some hot tea and snacks for us, while others grabbed a lamp and helped us fix the tire. Unphased by the early hour, they all had a twinkle in their eye and a smile on their face. It was clear that they were not a rich family. In fact, you could classify them, by most definitions, as living in poverty. Yet, that night, they were rich with an abundance of service. They had the power to transform what would have been a dangerous and frustrating experience for us into a pleasurable encounter we will remember forever. Money could never buy that type of experience!

People confuse generosity with the act of giving money or physical items. Since most people believe that they never have enough of these scarce resources, generosity is often an impulsive and sporadic event, ignited more by circumstance or a sudden emotional occurrence.

However, if we shed our scarcity mindset and engage in small acts of service, being generous can, in fact, be quite simple and satisfying.

A recent paper published in Psychological Science shows that helping other people can increase feelings of "time affluence" and alleviate the perceived "time famine."[4] The research shows that spending time helping others makes people feel like they have done a lot with their time. This creates a domino effect: the more people feel they have done with their time, the more time they will feel they have. Spending time on others seemed to "expand the future," in contrast to spending time focused on oneself.

No one is unable to give, because giving is relative. You can choose what you give, based on what you have. Giving your time and energy can often be as meaningful as giving money or resources. You can give a smile, you can give forgiveness and you can extend a prayer to someone. As Khalil Gibran said, "You give little when you give of your possessions; it is when you give of yourself that you truly give."

Receiving is just as important as giving.

In day-to-day life, the act of giving holds more moral significance than the act of receiving. In fact, we often view receiving as a reflection of inadequacy on the part of the receiver. However, receiving is as important as giving— listening, witnessing, observing and paying attention are all

---

[4] Mogilner, Cassie, Zoë Chance, and Michael I. Norton. "Giving Time Gives You Time." Psychological Science 23, no. 10 (2012): 1233–38. https://doi.org/10.1177/0956797612442551.

part of receiving, and we cannot be truly spiritually open until we are as open to receiving as we are to giving. Receiving and giving are two sides of the same coin. One cannot exist without the other.

There are many reasons why we feel uncomfortable receiving. Some people feel they are weak or have failed when they must ask for help. However, if we seek help in areas where we are not particularly accomplished, we can learn and grow, while also giving other people a chance to serve.

Some people fear that if they accept something, they will owe something in return. But we all practice reciprocity at some point in our lives. For instance, if you receive help from someone, it is natural to want to help them in some way. One day, you will have a chance to return the favor.

Whether or not we acknowledge it, we receive daily without registering it. We receive the air we breathe, the sunlight we feel on our skin, the fruits and vegetables we harvest from nature, the love of the people who care for us. We receive the peace in our countries, given to us by many people who sacrificed their lives. We all stand on the shoulders of others who have brought our civilization to where it is today.

Try this: close your hand and make a fist. Can you receive now? Or will anything given to you slip away? Now, open that closed fist and bare your palm. With an open hand, you can give and receive. Giving allows you to receive and receiving allows you to give.

Serve in a way that empowers people.

Across the world, one billion people still live in poverty despite decades of handouts that have been directed to these populations. The best thing we can do is empower these people, rather than overpowering them. This can create sustainable, multi-generational change. It will allow these individuals to acquire independence, build their confidence, tap into their potential, preserve their dignity and become masters of their destiny.

You have likely heard the saying, "Give a man a fish and you feed him for a day. Teach a man to fish, and you feed him for a lifetime." Giving a handout may provide temporary relief, e.g., "giving someone a fish." But service that comes from a place of abundance and humility can empower the recipient. Providing a hand-up can have a long-term effect, e.g., "teaching a person how to fish." While handouts such as signing a large donation check are required and necessary, hand-ups will bring you an inner sense of fulfillment when you see the beneficiaries use their agency to help themselves in the long-term.

The best way to gain happiness is to give happiness.

While popular culture may imply that happiness comes from focusing on your own needs, research suggests the opposite: being generous can make you happier. For example, one survey of 632 Americans found that spending money on other people was associated with significantly greater happiness than spending money on oneself, regardless of income.[5] This is true even from a young age: one study found that toddlers exhibited more happiness when giving treats to a puppet than when receiving treats themselves.[6]

---

5 "The Science of Generosity - Phase II." John Templeton Foundation, n.d. https://www.templeton.org/es/discoveries/the-science-of-generosity.

6 Aknin, Lara B., J. Kiley Hamlin, and Elizabeth W. Dunn. "Giving Leads to Happiness in Young Children." PLoS ONE 7, no. 6 (2012). https://doi.org/10.1371/journal.pone.0039211.

Survey data from 136 countries showed that people who had given to charity in the past year reported greater happiness than those who had not, regardless of their household income, age, gender, marital status, education and food inadequacy.[7] In fact, the happiness derived from donating to charity was on par with the level of happiness associated with a doubling of one's household income.

Giving is instantaneous. You feel innately good the moment you give. If you have ever helped someone, whether in a big or small way, you know what this feels like. Happiness is like a shadow: the more you follow it the more it escapes you. But the more you walk away from it, it follows you!

---

[7] Aknin, Lara B., Christopher P. Barrington-Leigh, Elizabeth W. Dunn, John F. Helliwell, Justine Burns, Robert Biswas-Diener, Imelda Kemeza, Paul Nyende, Claire E. Ashton-James, and Michael I. Norton. "Prosocial Spending and Well-Being: Cross-Cultural Evidence for a Psychological Universal." Journal of Personality and Social Psychology 104, no. 4 (2013): 635–52. https://doi.org/10.1037/a0031578.

Reflection Questions

- What are some examples of times when serving or sharing your time, skills or resources has created happiness for you?

  _____

  _____

  _____

  _____

- When you view service as an opportunity rather than a burden, how do you feel?

  _____

  _____

  _____

  _____

- What are some benefits you have derived from giving?

  _____

  _____

  _____

  _____

- What are some things you have received from others that you could be grateful for?

  _____

  _____

  _____

  _____

- Do you graciously accept a compliment, feedback or a gift? If not, why not?

- Do you ask for help when you need it?

- What are some of the most abundant areas of your life that you could share with others?

How to Get Started

- Give something daily, no matter how little—your time, knowledge, wisdom, resources, a prayer, positive vibes or energy. Start today. Make someone happy with a smile, kind word or helping hand. Pay close attention to how you feel when you do this. Write down a few ideas here.

  _____
  _____
  _____
  _____

- Treat every giving request as an opportunity instead of a burden. Show deep appreciation for those who come to you for a helping hand by treating them with utmost respect, dignity, reverence and making them feel special. Write out a few ways you can begin to look at giving this way.

  _____
  _____
  _____
  _____

- Express gratitude for everything you receive from others and the environment around you. Send a note of thanks to someone who has shown you generosity or someone you appreciate today. Write down what you'll say in the note below.

  _____
  _____
  _____
  _____

- Seek out an opportunity to mentor or coach someone, whether at work or home. Strive to empower your mentee rather than overpower them. Write down a few people you might be able to mentor or ways you might be able to find a mentee.

PART 2

Story:
Millennial Wisdom

There were few people at the McDonald's: a family with two children ordering a Happy Meal, a couple of women going over some papers, three teenagers having colas, and an older gentleman with a coffee, working on a crossword puzzle. Steve ordered the cheapest coffee on the menu and took a seat near the window.

He decided to use the washroom before the coffee came. There was just one tiny restroom with barely enough space to enter and close the door. He washed his hands and tried to clear the mud stains off his white shirt. But it only darkened and spread the dirt. He leaned forward to get some soap when he spotted a gold watch lying behind the dispenser.

It was a woman's timepiece, quaint and old-fashioned, with a roman dial and a slim, matte-gold strap.

Just a week ago, if he'd found a watch, he would have left it there, figuring that it was not his problem. But something in the last few days had expanded his idea of personal boundaries. He took the watch to the counter and informed the attendant.

The man held the watch in the air and called out to check

if it belonged to anyone there.

A woman leaped out of her chair, "It's mine!" she screamed excitedly.

"Oh dear ... looks like I forgot it in the washroom. Thank you," she said, reaching the counter.

The attendant pointed towards Steve. "You must thank Sir. He found it."

Steve smiled, raising his arms in mock surrender.

"Thanks ... Mr. ...?"

"Steve ... Steve Harmon."

"I am Ananya. It's my grandmother's watch," she said, clasping it gently around her wrist. "I am normally not so careless."

"It happens."

"We were about to leave. Had you not seen it, I might have lost it forever. So, thank you again."

"My pleasure."

Ananya and her colleague collected their knapsacks and headed back to the counter for a coffee to go. At the same time, Steve was there asking the attendant if they happened to keep bus timetables or route maps on hand for visitors like him.

The women whispered among themselves. Then, Ananya approached Steve.

"Where do you want to go?"

"Dharamsala," he replied.

"We will be passing the intercity bus stand. If you want, we can drop you there."

"Thanks, that would be great!" Any money he could save till he reached Dharamsala would be a plus.

With his coffee in a takeout cup, he followed them out to a small red hatchback. The women sat in the front, and Steve clambered into the back seat, next to a pile of fabric swatches and hardbound books of design patterns.

At Steve's request, they stopped at Jaimal's store, where Michelle had finally left the contact number of the person who would hand over the funds and documentation to Steve in Dharamsala.

It was late afternoon, and the traffic made its way forward sluggishly. They skirted around cattle and a noisy marriage procession whose guests were dancing around a bridegroom seated on a white horse dressed in a red and gold saddle. Street children danced alongside the procession as it passed a row of homeless people squatting on the pavement under blue plastic tarpaulin shelters. A Mercedes Benz waited alongside a handcart. Company buses dropped employees home. There were stray dogs everywhere.

Coming to India was like going down a rabbit hole and discovering several alternate universes, all somehow co-existing without collision.

The women curiously inquired if Steve was here to visit the Golden Temple. Their curiosity gave him a chance to tell them the entire chain of events. They intently listened to his harrowing story. Sometimes they were silent, and sometimes, they murmured to each other in the local dialect.

The car arrived at the bus station, but the two women were still talking among themselves. As Steve was about to open the car door, Ananya's colleague, Shruti, turned around and motioned for him to stop. "Steve, we don't do this often—I mean, women in India don't normally give lifts to strangers ... especially men ... so we didn't bring this up the first time we met. But ..."

"Yes, Shruti here wanted to make sure you were not a criminal on the prowl," Ananya added, rolling her eyes in the overhead mirror.

"But it looks like you have been the victim so far," Shruti

continued, shrugging her shoulders.

"I don't understand ..." Steve replied with a confused look.

Shruti sighed, then offered their proposal. "We are on our way to Palampur. And if you want, we can drop you off at Dharamsala."

"Are you sure? I wouldn't want to impose ..."

"It's OK ... it's only a four-hour ride," said Ananya. "We should be there by late evening."

The trio had been on the road for an hour when they decided to stop at a small roadside stall for some cardamom and ginger chai. They sipped the hot chai in clay cups, which added sweet, smoky earthiness to the tea. The evening had grown colder, and the landscape had shifted from vast golden fields to small hills and shrubs sprouting from rocky terrain.

"So, do you live in Palampur?" asked Steve.

"No, we are going there for a week-long training workshop for local artisans. Our company provides design, marketing, technical and organizational support to rural artisans, to help them develop their craft and market their products on a global scale," Ananya replied proudly.

"A design workshop for rural women?"

"Yes! There are countless villages and towns across India with local artists who are so talented, but they lack exposure and training. They are not able to use their craft to better their lives.

"Each region here has a distinct form and weave," Ananya continued excitedly. "However, most don't know what designs or color combinations work in the global market, or about current trends and what is marketable. But we have seen that, with just a few months of training and a few interventions, they quickly grasp what's needed and start creating products that can easily fetch more than double the current price. So instead of simply helping them with funds, we believe in equipping them with skills and knowledge, which can be very empowering."

"So, it's like the adage about teaching people how to fish," Steve said with a smile.

"Exactly," Ananya nodded.

"So … have you always been teaching fashion?" Steve asked.

"We are fashion design graduates. Shruti here is a graduate of Parsons, while I am a National Institute of Design grad."

"Impressive … but shouldn't you both be working at big fashion houses?"

"We did … for some time. Shruti was in Paris for two years. And I was with LVMH in Delhi. But after a while, the work stopped being fun. I mean, it's not like we were creating any great meaning or value. Yes, we had fantastic salaries, work benefits, international trips, and so on. But somehow, we were not making much difference to either our lives or the lives of others. We worked hard during the week and then partied equally hard on weekends. It was just about us all the time."

"And life looks very small when it's just about you," Shruti said, placing her cup on a tray table beside the stall's garbage bin.

The three made their way back to the car.

"So, what made you switch?" Steve asked.

"In my case, probably 'why' I made the switch is the more relevant question. I did it because I saw something I believed in," Shruti replied. "Mainly, the strength of a collective movement.

"I happened to meet the founder of our company at an

exhibition in Paris. I was fascinated by the diverse range of textiles she was showcasing—all created by separate groups of rural women spread across India who came together under one umbrella to unleash a fury of design. Women who had never even met before were now exchanging ideas, discussing weaves, mixing patterns to create something so remarkable and beautiful. I wanted to be a part of this art conglomerate. So, when she offered me a job, I packed my bags and came back."

Steve was intrigued. "Who's the owner of this company?"

"There are multiple owners. The company is owned by many small artisans across India," Ananya said.

"You mean like a cooperative?"

Shruti nodded. "Yes, exactly. It's run primarily to provide an essential service for the women rather than purely for-profit motives.

"When our founder decided to start the company, no bank was willing to give her a loan, especially because she would need to have sizable collateral for them to even entertain the idea. But instead of dropping the idea, she turned to the weavers and craftspeople and offered them equity. Each artisan invested a nominal amount. Combined with her own savings and investments from friends, they built up a sizable seed fund to start the company. Today, we are a community-owned business of 3,000 artisans from remote villages and regions across India. About 2,200 artisans are direct shareholders. Our turnover last year was about $1.5 million." Shruti was beaming.

"And you, Ananya? What was your 'why' for making the switch?"

"It's all about acknowledging my roots," she explained.

On my annual breaks, I usually visit my grandmother in our native village, where she is the head of the local governing body. This time, I spent a lot of time with a small women's cooperative she had recently started. They took me to the village fair. I had been to plenty of village fairs, but this time, armed with my design gaze, I saw so much more. The range of textiles, embroidery, color combinations, workmanship … it was stupendous! And these women were not even formally trained. Just skills and genius that had carefully been passed on for generations.

"And I realized I was also a product of this milieu. What I call *'my talent,' 'my genes,' 'my eye for design'*—on many levels, it is a product of the collective contribution of my village people, who had survived against all odds for centuries and still managed to preserve our art. But now, this art was dying. Middlemen were buying their work at rock-bottom prices and selling them in cities for huge profits while these artists still lived hand to mouth. Their children could not afford to carry on. But I could! I was one of the lucky few who could afford a good education and enjoy my success. To ignore this legacy and walk back to my life felt wrong."

"That's true," Shruti agreed. "You do feel you are complicit somehow if you selfishly ignore this tradition," Shruti added.

"But it must not have been easy," Steve probed. "This company, I assume, is quite small compared to the multinational brands you were working with earlier, correct?"

"Yes. The salary is half of what we made with those firms. But then again, just making money was never my sole purpose," explained Ananya.

Half? Steve was shocked. How is it possible to give up half of your financial security for a tie to tradition? He had to ask but tried to be polite about it so he would not insult the women.

"Isn't life too complex and varied to be encapsulated into a single purpose? Aren't there multiple purposes at different points in life?"

"Of course, there are different needs and goals at different times. But there is one major purpose that speaks to your deepest desire—your reason for being. Suppose you didn't have to work for a living. What would your contribution be to the world that would make you happy?" Shruti asked without really seeking an answer.

"I know I want to create something of value," she added. "Grow not only as an artist but also as a human being."

"Yeah ... create a positive impact in the world," Ananya confirmed.

She took in Steve's puzzled face. "Come on, don't look so cynical. You too must have started out with a dream, right? You must have had goals? I mean, look at you ... hotshot lawyer traveling across continents."

Steve smiled, "Yes ... of course, I do! I have a list of weekly, monthly, yearly, five-yearly and even decade-long goals. But I don't think any of them are so ... esoteric."

Ananya laughed. "Yes, our aspirations may come across as esoteric. But they are also very tangible and practical. The number of people we have worked with over the last three years, the range of work we have had the opportunity to be a part of, the enormous challenges we encounter daily ... trust me, the experience has been invaluable and very grounding. If I learned fashion design in school, I learned life design out here in the field."

Shruti passionately joined in. "I remember the third batch we worked with—about 20 women from a village in Tamil Nadu ... we lived there for three months, preparing for their first exhibition. And the response we got ... amazing! From the profits, we were able to buy sewing machines for each one of them. The look of joy on their faces as they opened the boxes—it was priceless!"

"Ya, the feeling you get … much more fulfilling than just earning a salary," Ananya smiled at the memory.

"You know, the moments that make you gasp?" Shruti said, looking at Steve.

Steve stayed silent, thinking to himself. Yes, there had been moments, he recalled, long ago. The first few years when he worked just for the sheer joy of it—the pro bono cases, the excitement of research, the diverse challenges, the exhilaration of signing on new clients and completing projects. But this was not the case in recent years. In the last decade, he had been too busy competing with everyone else and playing to win while embellishing his small existence.

Steve broke his silence, "But surely you miss the big city life?"

"Yes, of course … we miss the Starbucks coffee, plush offices, business-class tickets, dinners at fancy restaurants, the high street shopping and watching Netflix all night," Shruti said with a sarcastic laugh. "In its place, we now have to sip a five-rupee tea in a meadow of wildflowers, sleep under a canopy of stars on the roof of a house, chat with new friends, play barefoot with children, learn embroidery from grandmothers … poor us!" she giggled.

"And it's not like we have completely broken away from our earlier lives," she continued. "Our clients are still some of the biggest brands. We keep moving between two worlds. But now, work doesn't feel empty."

"But aren't there moments when you regret making this choice?" he persisted, suddenly doubtful of his real motive for asking. Did he really want to know? Or was he trying to steer them into saying something that would justify the choices he had been making?

"Yes, sometimes, when I am meeting my old college friends and colleagues, when I see the size of their pay packages and their lifestyle, or when I am exhausted from trying to sleep a whole night in a rickety bus … it can get difficult."

"Then, what keeps you motivated?"

"For me, it's a goal. By the time I turn 35, I want to open a good school specifically aimed at promoting indigenous art and design for children from rural towns and villages. So many of them are not able to educate themselves due to language or economic barriers. I want to make sure the next generation of artists in India has opportunities their parents never had. And this job is my preparation for that dream," Ananya replied. "And when it gets difficult, I always remember what my grandmother used to say: treat every challenge like an adventure, and you will enjoy learning through every experience."

"For me," Shruti chimed in, "I go by a quote from my favorite painter, Picasso: 'the meaning of life is to find your gift; the purpose is to give it away.' And every morning, I set out to use my gift by giving it away."

"I think if you are clear about your purpose, your principles will guide you and keep you strong, whatever the circumstances," Ananya said. "We have this one life … it seems a terrible waste to while it away for a few temporary pleasures. I mean, when you are on your deathbed, what do you think will be most important to you?" Shruti said.

There was a moment of silence as they drove on.

"Why are you so quiet?" Ananya asked Steve.

"Nothing … you have just set me thinking about my own journey," he replied, quietly. "What if I have been navigating the wrong one all along?"

The initial goals he had set when he was starting out as a young lawyer were all about the money because it was the one thing his life had always lacked. He remembered staunchly believing that money would be his currency of freedom.

Freedom to make choices and lead the life he wanted. And it had that, no doubt about it.

The money had afforded him the freedom to enjoy the good life, to make risky decisions he would have never made otherwise, to own possessions he had only once dreamed about owning. But this freedom had gradually morphed into a booby trap, bondage of sorts and all his own making.

Now, buying the latest car was no longer a source of joy but a necessity—part of the constant pressure to keep up with his bombastic peers. And with every new possession came its own encumbrances. More insurance policies, property taxes, membership fees. An increasing array of gyms and cosmetic medical treatments. Every move he made was but a mere filler to retain his place in the society to which he was now beholden. The constant pressure to be seen as having it all, even if it meant giving up more than your all.

The money that was supposed to free him had, in fact, tied him down in ways he had never imagined. For example, had he been in Toronto, he would never have stopped to get out of his car to enjoy a cup of tea by the roadside. And if such a moment presented itself, it would be attached to a professional or commercial reason, never for personal satisfaction. That was just not his bag.

He was slowly realizing whatever you possessed, possessed you back.

But was money to blame? There were other rich people who didn't seem so miserable and forsaken. Theo, for example ... that chap never looked miserable.

So, what was the missing link? They were in the same business. And on the same success path. So why was Steve feeling so miserable? Had his life journey just been a waste of time?

No sooner had he asked that inner question than he heard

Ananya say, "Nothing goes to waste really, not if you are awake."

He looked at her, startled for a moment, wondering if she had overheard his thoughts somehow.

"When you look back at your life so far, don't you think every moment seems to have transpired to bring you to this very moment of learning? For example, look at us. We live completely different lives on two separate continents. What are the chances of us running into each other in a city we all have visited for the first time? What were the chances of you ever passing on a message to your boss through a shopkeeper in Amritsar?" Shruti said.

"Yes. It seems surreal … as if somebody has been scripting this."

"It's a part of you that's been scripting this to bring you to this point of awareness. But now is the real moment of truth. How you use this awareness to decide your path ahead. You can either ignore this and carry on as before or script a whole new story," Shruti said.

"Aren't you guys too young to be spreading so much philosophical wisdom?"

"We can't help it … we're idealistic millennials," Ananya chuckled.

"Is that a polite way of calling me old and stupid?" Steve asked in mock anger.

Significance:
P: for *Purpose*

> *"There are two great days in a person's life.*
> *The day you are born and the day you discover why."*
>
> —Mark Twain

In this chapter, Steve saw that Ananya and Shruti seem to have discovered and are following their life's purposes. This inspired him to reflect on how he might find his own true meaning and ambition. The interactions and experiences shared in this section highlight how finding a true purpose is key to advancing from success to significance. Therefore, Purpose is the second ingredient to infusing your SPARK.

Let's examine some other causes and effects around the concept of Purpose:

Having a true Purpose can improve (and extend) your life.

A wise person once said, "The purpose of life is to have a life of purpose." When your life has meaning, impact and significance—a goal larger than self—it leads to a strong purpose. When the ego disappears into a goal larger than self, true purpose manifests. You know you have found your purpose when you lose track of time, when you become so involved in what you are doing that you don't even notice that you are hungry or tired.

Research supports the idea that a sense of purpose in life can improve health and longevity. An article in Harvard Women's Health Watch highlighted a study showing an association between a strong sense of purpose in life and a lower risk of death from cardiovascular problems and blood conditions.[1] The authors found that, among a group of nearly 7,000 adults over age 50, those who scored highest on a scale that measured "life purpose" were less likely to die during the study period, compared with those who scored lower.

Similarly, a Japanese study assessed the concept of *ikigai*, which translates to "a life worth living." Study participants with an average age of 67 were followed for around seven years. The analysis showed a lower risk of death for participants with a high sense of purpose in life. After adjusting for other factors, mortality for participants reporting a strong sense of purpose or ikigai was about one-fifth lower than it was for others. A high sense of purpose in life was also related to a lower risk of cardiovascular events.[2]

---

1 "A Purpose-Driven Life May Last Longer." Harvard Health, September 1, 2019. https://www.health.harvard.edu/mind-and-mood/a-purpose-driven-life-may-last-longer.

2 Wolters Kluwer Health: Lippincott Williams and Wilkins. "Sense of purpose in life linked to lower mortality and cardiovascular risk." ScienceDaily. www.sciencedaily.com/releases/2015/12/151203112844.htm.

Start by looking inward.

Unlocking your true purpose is not easy. It requires heightened self-awareness, inward reflection on your experiences and your unique gifts, an awareness of what the world needs now and a deep understanding of your passions, values and interests. This process requires introspection, reflection, contemplation and self-acceptance.

Leadership expert Simon Sinek recommends that you "start with why" when identifying your purpose, whether for an organization or as an individual.[3]

The "why" is your reason for being and can inspire action. Sinek's theory is that successfully communicating the passion behind the "why" is a way to communicate with the limbic brain. This is the part of our anatomy that processes feelings such as trust, loyalty, and decision-making. When the "why" is clear, the "how" becomes easier.

Starting with why requires you to ask the following questions:

- Why am I doing what I am doing?

- What would happen if I did not do what I am doing?

- How does what I am doing help my purpose or create meaning, impact and significance?

Aim to achieve flow states.

In positive psychology, a flow state, also known colloquially as "being in the zone," is the mental state in which a person performing some activity is fully immersed in a feeling of

---

3 Sinek, Simon. Simon Sinek, n.d. https://simonsinek.com/.

energized focus, full involvement and enjoyment of the activity. This is not necessarily about the activity itself but how you conduct the activity. A flow state is achieved when what you are doing is aligned with your purpose.

Flow can be achieved through meditation, mindfulness, music, sport, poetry, learning or volunteering. Breath, movement and passion can also get you into a flow state. Benefits of "flow" include a greater sense of clarity, good feelings, happiness, lack of obstacles and a heavy sense of concentration.

Mihaly Csikszentmihalyi and Nakamura reached this conclusion by interviewing a variety of self-actualized, high-performing people, including mountain climbers, chess players, surgeons and ballet dancers.[4] These individuals become so engaged in their craft that they do not have the leftover capacity to think about their anxieties, pain, hunger, exhaustion or other challenges. Their identities disappear from their consciousness when they're in a flow state because they do not have the attention span to both perform this activity that requires all their concentration and to feel their existence.

Open your birthday gift (what you are born with!)

Og Mandino eloquently said, "A mulberry leaf touched with the genius of man becomes silk. A field of clay touched with the genius of man becomes a castle. A Cypress tree touched with the genius of man becomes a shrine. A cut of sheep's hair touched with the genius of man becomes raiment for a king … Today I will multiply my value a hundredfold."

---

4 "What Is a Flow State and What Are Its Benefits?" Headspace, n.d. https://www.headspace.com/articles/flow-state.

We have all come to this world with unique skills and gifts. To find and fulfill our purpose, we must open our birthday gifts and strive for the work we were born to do.

Unfortunately, most people don't know they have a gift. And even many who are aware that they may have a gift don't know what the gift is or how to find it. Some who are cognizant of their gift and feel they know how to find it lack the discipline to materialize it. Then, there are those who have the discipline to find their gift but lack the focus to optimize its use throughout the various facets of their lives.

What a tragedy it is that people go through their entire lives either never opening the miraculous gift buried inside them or never fully optimizing the gift when found!

Only you can be you! Be the best version of yourself.

Where are you on this journey? Have you opened your birthday gift yet? To discover this gift, ask yourself the following:

- What kind of work makes you happy? Or makes you come alive?
- If you could do anything in life and nothing could stop you from being extremely successful at it, what would you dare to do?
- What conversation about the life you've lived do you see yourself having with your Creator while on your deathbed? What would be the one WOW achievement you would share about your life?
- If there is *one* thing you must do (not hundreds) before your life ends, what would it be?
- What cause would you be most excited to serve, and where?
- Do you believe life has a great and noble calling—a lofty

and exalted Destiny? If so, how can you make your life lofty and exalted? What specific things do you need to do to achieve such an elevated state?

- Are purpose and principles anchors in your life? If not, what can you do to align your principles and provide meaning to yourself?

- Do you work on being the grandest version of yourself? If not, what would make you the grandest version of yourself?

- Life is not about You. It is about the impact you make on others. If you believe it is never too late to live your purpose, where can you make the highest impact?

Remember, only *you* can be *you*. Be your true self; everyone else is taken!

Learn to say "no" for a deeper "yes."

Crystal clarity of your goals comes from the ability to say "no" to items that are not aligned to your deeper "yes." Saying "no" to things that do not align with your goals, including your service, will free up time to focus on your deeper "yes."

If we were to accomplish hundreds of other objectives, but not our main purpose, we are destined to depart this world feeling incomplete. Rumi, the Sufi mystic, once wrote, "There is one thing in this world you must never forget to do. If you forget everything else and not this, there is nothing to worry about, but if you remember everything else and forget this, then you will have done nothing in your life."

Seek significance over success.

I have noticed around the world that people who spend their lives chasing typical ideals of success end up realizing that it is "significance" or meaning that they truly seek.

Pablo Picasso once recounted, "My mother said to me, if you are a soldier, you will become a General. If you are a monk, you will become the Pope. Instead, I was a painter and became Picasso." Finding your genuine purpose may mean following your heart to be your truest self, rather than chasing titles or other people's goals.

Let your authentic Purpose be your guide.

With a pure purpose in place, you will know where you are going and, most importantly, why you want to get there. Driven by the destination, you can allow your real purpose to forge your voyage with energy, meaning, gumption and love. With a sound purpose, you will lose track of time because you will act out of the absolute joy of making a difference for others, not only yourself.

As you pilot your ship, all of nature is on call, operating in silence to sync with your purpose. Every part of the Universe provides service and alignment to your goals. The air is fresher, giving healthy life to your breath; the sun is brighter, giving luminous light to help you find your way.

Your birthday gifts are intuitively tied to your purpose. Your challenge is to discover your purpose, commit to it and use the gifts the Universe has bestowed on you to fulfill it. When you accept the purpose you were born to execute, you can use your innate gifts to make a profound impact on life.

Once you find your truest purpose, infuse all your

activities with it, be they personal, business, familial, social or community-related. This not only creates congruence and harmony but also entrenches your purpose into your very being because you walk it, talk it, breathe it and sleep it.

It is never too late to live your absolute Purpose.

There is no time like the present to begin articulating and living your purpose. As Ralph Waldo Emerson is said to have once remarked, "What lies behind us and what lies before us are tiny matters, compared to what lies within us."

During the 2020 COVID-19 pandemic, a former British Army officer, Sir Thomas Moore (also known as Captain Tom), expressed his intention to raise £1,000 for heroic frontline healthcare workers by walking one hundred laps around his garden by his 100th birthday. Excited to help, his family leveraged the power of social media to seek donations.

Lo and behold, by his 100th birthday, he had amassed a donation fund of over £33 million (US$40 million)! A simple determination "to make tomorrow better than today" awoke a nation in lockdown to unite and take part in positive change during a very difficult time.[5]

If that wasn't enough, the distinguished war veteran went on to become the oldest person ever to score a number one single in the UK. His duet with Michael Ball, a cover of "You'll Never Walk Alone," reached the top of the charts and sold 82,000 copies, with all proceeds going to the National Health Service (NHS) Charities.

If a newly turned centenarian like Sir Tom Moore can

---

5 Burchell, Helen. "Capt Sir Tom Moore: How the Retired Army Officer Became a Nation's Hero." BBC News. BBC, February 2, 2021. https://www.bbc.com/news/uk-england-beds-bucks-herts-52324058.

unlock his true Purpose at the ripe old age of 99, it is surely never too late for any of us to do the same.

Find your deathbed WOW.

When Steve Jobs passed away in 2011, his sister said that before he died, he began his transition by looking at her. He then gazed at his children, then he turned his attention toward his life partner, and finally over their shoulders, past them all. It was at that point he uttered his final words: "OH WOW. OH WOW. OH WOW."[6]

What Jobs was WOW-ing at remains unclear, or clear only to those loved ones around him. But what we do know is that he had his own clear Purpose, and this final interaction was his way of showing his immense gratitude for all those who brought meaning to his life. Having a clear Purpose, pursuing it and achieving it can lead to a deathbed of WOWs. So, what would make you exclaim "WOW" on your deathbed?

You are here for a nobler purpose than just to survive—to eat, sleep, produce offspring and die. You are a miracle! You are unique, gifted, special and have something precious to contribute. There is no one like you in the entire world. You are distinct, rare and powerful! But your value and enormous power will shine brighter when you open your innate gift and discover your Purpose. Only then will you shine your light and inspire others to do the same.

---

6 Simpson, Mona. "A Sister's Eulogy for Steve Jobs." The New York Times. The New York Times, October 30, 2011. https://www.nytimes.com/2011/10/30/opinion/mona-simpsons-eulogy-for-steve-jobs.html.

REFLECTION QUESTIONS:

- Is your life currently meaningful and fulfilling? How would you define your true purpose in life?
  _____
  _____
  _____
  _____

- Think about a time when you felt you were in a flow state. Did time pass without you realizing it? Were you totally in the zone? What were you doing? How can this recollection inform and guide your life's purpose moving forward?
  _____
  _____
  _____
  _____

- What are the anchors and principles in your life that act as a foundation for your goals?
  _____
  _____
  _____

- What is your birthday gift? What is the one thing you must accomplish with your life?
  _____
  _____
  _____
  _____

- When you are dying and reflecting on your life, what would you like to be able to say about yourself?

- Are you living your life as the best version of you? If not, how will you change for the better?

HOW TO GET STARTED:

- Do something today that aligns with your Purpose. If you have not found your purpose yet, then explore the "Why" questions I laid out on page 51 to help you get closer to finding your purpose.

- Say "no" to one thing today that does not align with your deeper "yes."

- Do one thing today that brings out the best version of you. Continue this practice until it becomes an instinctual habit.

- Articulate what activities make you lose track of time and cultivate a flow state, so you are inspired to do more of it.

- Write down the one thing you would like to accomplish before you die.

  _____
  _____
  _____
  _____

PART 3

Story:
Apricot Man

Steve could not help but notice the mountains, which glowed a deep, smoky blue against the orange-and-purple-streaked sky. It had been a very long time since he was able to take in Mother Nature's grandeur. Back home, it was always go-go-go, with no time to breathe, let alone notice the beauty of a sunset.

The girls dropped him off by the market square. Before leaving, Ananya pulled out a duffel bag from under the car seat and took out a small black phone.

"Keep this. The phone number is on the back. It also has 1GB of free data. It will make it easier to speak to the person who is dropping the stuff off for you."

"I just can't accept this," Steve fumbled, struggling to find the right words.

"It is not a handout, if that is what you fear," she laughed. "These phones are only free for our artisans because many of the women in the villages don't own phones—only their husbands do. With a phone in hand, they feel more confident. Also, we are then but a quick phone call away to assist them when needed. So, this is technically company property.

"So, when you can, transfer the cost of the phone to the company account, and send me a message to confirm it's done, Ananya said. "I have messaged the account details to this number."

"But we have just met. You're taking a big leap of faith by doing this. I mean, what if I don't pay back the money?"

"Well, first off, it's no iPhone," she shrugged. "I'll simply wait for three days, then once I've confirmed you have stolen the phone, I'll make the payment myself, from my account, to avoid any issues."

"… and we'll probably never take a leap of faith again," Shruti added, sighing dramatically.

They all laughed.

Touched by all they did for him, he waited until the car disappeared into the evening light.

After taking a cursory walk around the market, he found quite a few lodges around the area. He selected the cheapest one, at 200 rupees per night.

After a quick snack of bananas and apples, he headed back to the lodge, a small blue building crammed between shops. He unlocked his door and entered a tiny room, dimly lit by a single white fluorescent light. There was a narrow, metal-framed cot, a table with an earthen pitcher, and a wooden chair with its seat missing, parked next to the only window in the room.

He pushed open the window shutters to see a small courtyard opening at the rear of the hotel. Two men dressed in only their boxer shorts, a light mist rising off their dark, gleaming bodies, were washing clothes under a running tap. After washing their clothes, they took a wash under the same tap. So *that* was the community washing area the hotel manager had whispered about. No way was he going down there! It was better to take a quick wash in the toilet instead.

But Steve soon discovered why the others had not considered that idea. The toilet was a tiny four-foot-by-four-foot room, with barely enough space to get in and close the door behind you.

It was an old-fashioned toilet, the flush mechanism an ancient yellowed ceramic tank that hung above the toilet. There was no sign of toilet paper anywhere. But luckily, he still had the wad of tissues he had picked up from Starbucks in his back pocket. He instinctively decided to pull on the rusty metal chain clanging below the flush. This action was immediately met by a sudden noisy plume of water, so loud that it would undoubtedly alert everyone on the floor about his bathroom exploits. After inspecting the water quality from the small tap, he had to admit that if he didn't want to smell like a muddy, manure-soaked pig, he would have to go down to the courtyard to take that wash after all.

However, he decided he would go there as late in the day as possible, just to avoid being seen. So, at 30 minutes past midnight, when the floor seemed to be at its quietest, he softly slipped out of his room. With his shirt and trousers gathered in his arms, Steve scampered down to the tap.

By that time, a full moon had appeared majestically in the night sky, further illuminating the activity he had so wanted to get done in the dark.

But there was no other option. He sat on his haunches in the courtyard by the running tap, shivering in the frigid air, trying to clean the mud stains off his only shirt with a tiny piece of soap that had long ago lost its ability to lather. He berated himself for not buying a bar of soap from the market when he had the chance. It was now also too late to go back to the manager to ask for anything more. But all said and done, at least he was alone—no one around to share in his misery.

And then, he looked up and froze.

There was an entire floor of people peering out of their room windows, some with their mouths open, some grinning, some laughing, but all whispering—all of them transfixed by the sight of a light-skinned foreigner in his bright blue boxers printed with yellow smiling suns, washing clothes in the gleaming moonlight.

Talk about bringing down a man from the 48th floor. He had really reached rock bottom! His embarrassment was clear for all to see.

So, he did the only thing that came to mind. He looked up and waved.

And to his surprise, a few of them happily waved back.

He had never felt so exposed and yet so free.

By the end of his second round of washing, his newfound fans were pumping their fists and cheering him on. A few even whistled when he finally hung his dripping shirt out to dry on the clothesline.

When he finally collapsed onto the bed at 2 a.m., he was way too tired to be bothered by the small family of cockroaches scuffling behind his pillow. Oh, how far he had fallen, he thought for a moment before drifting off to sleep.

When he woke up, it was already eight o'clock. After taking a quick wash and donning his clean clothes, he called Nadia, the woman Michelle had referred him to—the one who would deliver his new cards and some much-needed cash. She had been delayed due to a landslide from more torrential rains and wouldn't be able to meet until 4 p.m. They agreed to meet at a popular coffee shop in McLeod Ganj, a small hilly suburb, about two miles from the main Dharamsala town square.

Given the late meeting time, he had the entire day to himself. He came out of the room to see a small group of men sitting in the corridor of the veranda, sipping tea and eating what looked like buns. Their eyes immediately flickered in recognition from the previous night, and a few gestured to him to join them. One of them poured him a steaming cup of tea in a small glass from a large aluminum jug he kept on a stool.

By this time, Steve had lost his natural hesitation to accept things, so why not also welcome the bun, too? He proceeded to dip it into the hot sweet tea like the others, then munched on it quickly before the wet piece had a chance to slip back into the cup.

After thanking them in gestures, he checked out of his room and decided to walk to McLeod Ganj.

He slowly strolled up the hill, with nothing except the envelope he had now wrapped in a plastic bag and 220 rupees in his pocket. For the first time in many years, he felt free. Void of any tension about finding a parking spot, remembering to lock up the house or picking out the right suit for the occasion. All of that felt menial now. Unnecessary, even.

The market was a collage of colors with its brightly lit cafes and fruit carts, shops selling nuts and teas and Tibetan handicrafts, shawls and scarves. After ten minutes, the street widened into a winding road, perched delicately between a mountain on one side and a stream gurgling in the valley below. It was a bright, sunny day, and the tang of pine and moss lingered in the air, while the asphalt was littered with intensely red flowers from the rhododendron trees now in full bloom along the edge of the road.

Traffic was still sparse, with just a few tourists and monks in red robes enjoying the fresh morning air.

He had decided to have breakfast after reaching McLeod Ganj, but the fresh mountain air and the climb had made him ravenous. So, when he spotted a tree sprinkled with peach-flecked yellow and green apricots, his stomach rumbled.

He picked up the first decent-sized stone he could find and aimed it at a section of the tree where some fruit hung. But the apricots were small, and the stone failed to make contact. He attempted several throws but with no success.

By now, he was no longer just hungry but *hangry!* His ex-wife always pointed this out when he became irrationally angry after skipping a meal. To have his patience tested by a stupid tree was not what he needed right now. He grabbed an overhanging branch, broke it off, and used it to jab and pull down the higher branches to lunge at the apricots. But he only succeeded in breaking several small limbs and raining a shower of leaves. His actions yielded only one tiny apricot, still hard and green.

He was about to take his next shot at a branch when someone shouted from behind.

"Stop … how much more damage will you do?!"

He turned around to see a tall, stocky man holding bags in both hands, standing several feet behind him. He looked like he was in his mid-60s. He had a robust, ruddy complexion, framed with stark white hair and a white beard. His eyes were intelligent and bright. He also looked vaguely familiar.

"Wait," the man sighed, gently resting the bags against the trunk of the tree and motioning him to step aside.

Linking his arms behind his back, the man took a short, slow walk around the tree, stopping, peering at it closely. After completing a few rounds, he picked his spot, rolled back his sleeves, then extended his arm and gently tapped one section of a branch. Two apricots immediately fell, rolling down among the dry leaves below. He circled around once again and tapped at another branch, and a few more fruit dropped into a bed of leaves.

Steve watched the ritual, with his jaw hanging open.

Gathering the fruits in his hands, the man offered them to Steve. "This should be enough for you."

"That was so smooth. How did you …? I have been trying for the last ten minutes to nail just one."

"Violence is not the answer. Understanding is."

"Excuse me?" Steve said, confused.

"If you had spent a few minutes observing the tree, you would have known which apricots you could guide down to the ground," the man said. "You see, when the tree senses the fruit is ripe, it usually drops it on its own. At best, it needs a gentle nudge. You don't need to throw stones or beat it with sticks."

Steve was tempted to say something, but he kept quiet, his mouth salivating for the bright, tumescent fruits in his hands.

"It so happens that it's not just you who yearns for the fruit. The tree wants to give it up, too. For you, it's sustenance, and for the tree, it's the propagation of seeds."

Steve laughed.

The man sighed. "Now go on … enjoy the fruit. And when you are done, fling the seeds in the valley below. Give this tree the opportunity to thank you back," the man said, folding his hands and bowing to the tree.

"Wait … are you actually bowing to the tree?"

"I am bowing to consciousness, thanking it for gifting us the fruit."

"Consciousness … in the tree?" Steve snorted.

"In everything—this tree, that rock, the birds, you, me … we are all vibrating with the same consciousness."

"Seriously … even this rock?" Steve chuckled.

"Yes … of course," the man said, his face serious. "The quality of consciousness and its expression might vary, but we all dance to the same song."

Steve laughed, shook his head, and looked up at the tree.

And for a moment, it appeared as if the tree was laughing back at him, its branches swaying merrily in the wind, the leaves shimmering green and yellow in the golden sunlight.

"So next time, remember, young man," the man said, "before you use force or demand anything, just spend some time observing the situation with fresh eyes. You might discover that what you seek is also seeking you."

"Hmm, beautiful philosophy," Steve replied, chomping on the fruit, its sweet-tart juices filling his mouth with music. Apricots had never tasted so delicious before. "That might work for nature … but out there … in the real world … not very practical."

"Hmm … so where is this 'out there' located, exactly?" the man asked.

Before he answered, he decided to introduce himself. "Hi, I'm Steve," he said, extending the hand not covered in apricot juice. "I'm from Canada … Here on business. And the 'out there' I was referring to is the business world."

"Hmm … business … so you're a big man, yes? And outside the humble realm of this existence, yes?" the man snorted.

"I didn't mean to offend you," Steve replied. "My only intention was to highlight that you can't function like this in real life, especially business. It can't be all nice and rosy … Out there, you need to have a killer instinct."

"And who are you planning to kill … with this instinct?"

"What?" asked Steve with a crumpled, confused face.

"Where are you planning to use this killer instinct? Who do you want to kill? Your customers?"

"Well … I …" He wasn't sure how to reply. Steve had never thought about it like that.

"And once you kill your customers, who are you planning to sell to the next time? Or do you plan to keep moving from market to market, leaving destruction in your wake? And what happens when you have killed all your customers?"

"OK … I don't mean to kill customers. But what about the competition? You need to eliminate the competition."

The man shook his head sadly. "Be careful what you wish for. It might come true. It was nice meeting you," he replied, bending down to pick up his bags.

But now, Steve's ego was activated and gushing in full force. What gave this man the right to be so condescending? It made Steve feel a little foolish. OK, so the man had some skills with trees. But the business realm was Steve's playground, and he was not going to cede that hallowed ground so easily.

"Wait … where are you going?" Steve called after the man in a confident tone.

"Going home … up there … in McLeod Ganj," the man replied calmly, pointing up at an elevated neighborhood in the distance.

"Oh good, I need to get to McLeod Ganj as well. I can help you with these bags," Steve said.

"Are you sure?" the man asked, only to be polite—he already knew the answer.

"Yes. You were kind enough to stop and help me with breakfast. The least I can do is help you up the hill."

"Great … here," the man promptly replied, instantly handing him not one but both his loaded bags.

Steve fumbled but recovered quickly. The bags were heavy, packed with books, but nothing Steve couldn't handle. He was a beast in the gym and easily bench-pressed 200 pounds. So how bad could a few pounds of paper be?

The man walked fast, and Steve clambered up, falling in line with him.

"So, you didn't answer my question," Steve said.

"What question?"

"About eliminating competition. Surely you need to have a killer instinct for that."

"Eliminating competition ... so that means you think only you should have the right to run your business? No one else? Am I correct?"

Steve shrugged. "Well ... kind of."

"That to me, my friend, sounds like a dictatorship. And we have all seen how dictators end up."

"How did dictators come into a conversation about business?"

"You described them. I only supplied the word," the man said.

Steve squinted, replaying the words in his mind.

"Let's forget this word 'dictatorship,' since you find it upsetting," the man continued, chuckling. So, what will you do when there is no longer any competition? Start making a killing from your customers? You have to use that killer instinct somewhere."

"Yes, why not? Kill competition and become the market leader," Steve replied adamantly.

"For how long?"

"What do you mean? As long as possible," Steve replied, resting one bag on the ground to free up a hand and push a few dangling hairs, now damp with sweat, away from his face.

"So, you agree, this market leadership cannot continue indefinitely?"

Steve shrugged his shoulders, not fully understanding.

"See that river flowing below, cutting through those rocks? That blade of grass breaking out of that wall. That's life. And it always finds a way."

"Meaning?" Steve asked, still confused.

"Meaning ... you might stomp out the competition for

some time, but somebody, somewhere, will eventually find a way to simply change the rules of the game. As Uber did with the taxicab industry. Then, what will you do? There will be no more making a killing since all your cannon fodder will have migrated to the new market. And if you spend all your time killing competition, when do you plan to run your business?"

"Well, that's a very simplified way of looking at it."

"It's only when you simplify your ideas and spell them out that you see them for what they truly are: gold or garbage. And all that killing … how do you think it will affect you? You think you will escape it unscathed? No, you won't," the man said, walking at a brisk pace. "Every action creates a consequence. And one of the consequences is that it will change you. Eventually, it will turn you into a dictator, whether you like it or not. And dictators throughout history may have lived lives celebrating power, but never happiness. So be careful of what seeds you sow. Your misery, your happiness—it's all your creation, your responsibility."

"OK … Maybe using the phrase 'killer instinct' is not cool. But you must agree about the competition? It eats into your business. It's one of the main obstacles in every business," Steve argued, now panting slightly with each step, the weight of the books slowly feeling heavier than when he first picked up the bags.

"What is your business goal?" the man asked

"Making profits by serving our customers, of course," Steve replied without hesitation.

The man immediately stopped, cupped his hands, and looked up at the sky, muttering something under his breath.

"What … was … that?" Steve asked sarcastically.

"Oh … just had to say a little thank you prayer. We have made a monumental shift … from killing customers to serving them," the man chortled.

Steve couldn't resist laughing along. But soon, he went back to making his point. "But seriously, the obstacle ... competition still remains. You don't know how tough it is in the workplace and marketplace."

The man turned to him. "Oh ... is that so?" Then, leaning toward him, the man whispered, "Just because you don't see someone looking frustrated or anxious, you shouldn't assume they have never lived in what you call your 'real world.'"

"I didn't mean it that way," Steve stammered. "And if you ... you ... don't mind my asking ... how much further do we have to go?" Steve said, his shoulders heaving as he panted.

The road had become steep, and the sun was now overhead in a brilliant blue sky, running rivulets of sweat down Steve's shirt.

"Oh ... just a small stretch now," the man answered.

Steve nodded. The man made no offer to take back his bags or ask if he was tired. He merely marched on.

Steve quickened his pace to fall in line again. "What I meant was, in my office, I am competing with two others, Susan and Narayen, for the same position."

"Is your goal about you or them?" the man replied.

"What do you mean?"

"Ever seen Usain Bolt sprinting? When he runs in a race, he only has eyes for the finish line, his goal. He never looks behind. In the same way, your goal should be your only focus. You should work with such intensity and totality that your very task becomes the goal. Outperforming your competition then becomes but a by-product of your action, not the goal."

Steve thought about it for a while, "I like that ... by-product of your action and not the goal."

"So, what's your goal?" asked the man.

"Like I said, becoming the COO!" Steve said excitedly,

stopping under a tree to put the bags down and catch his breath.

This time, the man stopped with him.

"Now be clear, is your goal becoming the COO? Or is it defeating Susan and Narayen? Because the path is different for each. And if you are not clear about your goal, you might keep running in circles and going nowhere."

"Becoming the COO," Steve answered, starting to walk again. "That's my goal."

"And what will you do once you become the COO? What is it about this position that attracts you?"

"A lot of things," Steve said confidently. "It will empower me to explore new possibilities for providing great service to our customers; build and grow an excellent team; explore new business opportunities; earn good profits. But most of all, it will allow me to help my company lead with ethical and responsible practices that further enhance our market positioning."

"Oh my lord," the man laughed. "You know, when you said COO, the term seemed so small. But now I see ... your role is a massive enterprise in the making. I think the only thing you missed was world peace."

Steve smiled sheepishly.

"Don't be embarrassed. You are on the right track. Unless you are attracted to a bigger vision, where your base idea of becoming the COO can disappear into a larger objective of helping those around you grow and prosper, your goal will not succeed. And if it does prevail, it will not be very satisfying. We are all interconnected. The more you are of service to the world, the greater your success."

"But what if my competition creates obstacles? People can be ruthless."

"Hmmm ... the pot calling the kettle black. Remember your killer instinct? Hunters shouldn't be surprised at becoming the hunted. Like you, there are many who believe in and celebrate this killer instinct."

"But even if I change my thinking, the world will not … and I have to defend myself."

The man looked at Steve. "Nobody said eliminating killer instinct means eliminating survival instinct. Use your intelligence to resolve your challenge or, better still, create a new opportunity out of it. But if your response is creating obstacles for them in return, then let me tell you, none of you are going to fill that position. Once you start creating trouble for each other, your goal shifts from performance to troublemaking. And no company rewards a troublemaker."

"Fair point," Steve exclaimed.

And once you achieve your goal, don't become too attached to it."

"What do you mean?" Steve nearly shouted. "Am I not supposed to enjoy my success?"

"Of course, enjoy. Celebrate it. But then, don't get stuck there. There are far bigger worlds to explore and experience. Often, people achieve a goal and become so attached to it that they expend all their energy trying to preserve the sensation of that single achievement, instead of expanding their world."

The bag of books weighed him down, never mind the depth of this conversation. "How much further?" Steve asked.

"Oh … just around the bend," the man pointed to yet another curve in the road.

"But if you don't love your goal, how will you summon the passion for accomplishing it?" Steve asked quietly, trying to find the breath to speak.

"Hmmm, looks like you are confusing love with attachment."

"Aren't they the same? Or can one exist without the other? If I become detached from my goal, won't I also lose my desire for it? If I don't own it, how will I love it?"

"Detachment does not mean you cannot own anything. It means nothing owns you. The kind of love you are referring to is motivated by possessiveness, domination. In this possession, you feel a certain safety and stability. It becomes your comfort zone. And consequently, you want this comfort zone to continue indefinitely. So, you cling to it. But this clinging also breeds anxiety and jealousy. It creates conflict whenever you perceive any threat to it. It keeps you constantly worried about your future when you should be focusing your attention on what's present now."

Steve grimaced, "How so?"

"Imagine you just crossed a river in a boat. What do you do when you reach the other side?"

"Get off the boat and carry on?" Steve responded, surprised by how obvious the answer was. The man seemed to constantly be contradicting him or speaking in riddles, and now he was asking a question this simple?

"Well, attachment would insist you carry that boat with you because you should be scared you might not find a boat on your way back, and letting it go would pose a great risk to your survival. But under these conditions, you will only tire yourself. Your attachment becomes a burden that you must keep dragging along. It slows you down. So instead of getting attached to designations and possessions, explore how best you can use your position and assets to open new possibilities and aspire for higher goals."

"But doesn't that also get tiring ... this endless chasing of variable goals?" Steve, already tired as it is, imagined that this sounded exhausting.

"Not if your goals help expand your life. Humans, by their evolutionary nature, yearn for more, for expansion. There is always something more attractive on the horizon, isn't there? Something that calls out to you compels you to move forward, to strive for something more valuable. No other animal endeavors for anything more than basic survival and comfort. It is only the human-animal who dares to aspire, to dream for a better job, a higher position, a bigger home ... to expand their experience of life."

"Sometimes bigger is simply bigger, not better," Steve said.

"Precisely ... and people who can't see that remain stuck in material possessions and suffer. The joy of expansion is not in owning more but becoming more. That which calls out to you is not a possession or an object—it is your deepest calling to expand, to be a part of something greater, more profound than your current experience. That's the meaning of expanding your vision. As soon as you clarify your higher purpose and aim to serve something larger than yourself, your attachment goes as far as using the boat to cross the river. Once there, you can dock it without fear of material loss. And people, who understand this, live magical lives."

It had been an hour since they started their ascent up the hill. The man turned left into a narrow path leading further up the mountain. Then, out of nowhere, the road suddenly flattened and opened into a small clearing. There, in the shade of the great pines, stood a grey stone bungalow with a small lawn and a row of neatly trimmed wild rose bushes flanking the border. A mulberry tree dangled over the roof of the house, littering the red tiles with purple berries, attracting a swarm of life—bees, butterflies, and tiny hummingbirds, their taut little bodies glistening in dark blue velvet as they hovered, flapped and dipped over the fallen fruit.

The man unlocked the door and invited him inside. It was a small room, neatly arranged with just two armchairs around a roughly hewn oak table near the window. A long, olive-green bookshelf stood against one wall. At the other end, a single cot with a red-and-rust-yellow bedspread stood under another window. A saxophone case and a Bose music system were resting on a cabinet by the wall. Two other rooms opened off it.

The man motioned Steve to leave the bags in a wicker basket near the door.

"You have good stamina for someone who doesn't live in the hills. It's difficult for people to walk such a distance with two heavy bags up an incline."

"To be honest, it was very tiring. But our conversation kept me going. And whenever I thought I couldn't carry on, you kept saying we were just around the corner." Steve, peeking out of the window, continued, "But now I see we covered a lot of 'just around the corners'!"

The man laughed. "I had to provide some hope to help make your climb less difficult. Please, have a seat. I'll pour you a nice cup of mint tea … hope you like tea?"

"Yes, please, thank you!" Steve said, taking a seat by the window. "But isn't that hope you provided just a form of denial?"

"Hope does not mean turning a blind eye to reality or living in self-neglect. It is about accepting the situation as it is and deciding to find a better way to deal with it. It's about showing up, even when you are afraid you may fail. It's about working through the tough stuff, the painful stuff, and still carrying on because you know you are stronger than you think you are. But of course, hope alone is never enough. You have to apply focus and persistence," the man said, entering the kitchen.

"Yes … but I have seen a lot of people using hope as an excuse to not do anything in the present," Steve said.

"You are right. Hope is not a crutch to support a dream for which you intend to do nothing. It is a catalyst. On its own, it might not amount to much, but as the driver of all the other ingredients— energy, focus, persistence, intelligence—it makes it all come together very powerfully. It is the sweet sauce of resilience. Oh, that reminds me ... I made soup today. Would you like to have a bowl after your tea?"

"That would be great." Steve was starving after all the hiking and debating. "But don't you think hope also leads to disappointment? If you don't hope, there is no danger of losing whatever it is you may be hoping for."

"Hmmm ... it sounds like someone's hopes have been dashed," the man called from the kitchen.

"I meant in general, in life. Every day, people have their hopes dashed. Their dreams broken. And it hurts much more when you have been long hoping for something."

"Let's not focus too much on other people for now," the man remarked over the whistle of the kettle. "We can't comment on their situation without knowing them or their personal stories. Tell me about you instead."

"Sure." Steve was relieved. Finally, something where the man couldn't know more than him. "For the last six months, I've been working on a big business deal, and just when it was about to close and I could finally claim victory, I was summoned to travel here. Where that deal ends up or whether I will bear the fruits of my labor is in the balance."

"Ah ... victory," the man answered, bringing out a tray with two cups of tea and a pot of sugar.

"Sometimes, our idea of victory and the Universe's idea of victory can be two very different things. Don't be in a rush ... you don't know what foundation those six months of work have laid. While you may see all your effort going to waste in this deal, life might have bigger deals in place for you."

"Maybe. But so far, the Universe has been quiet," Steve

shrugged, accepting the cup of tea. "Nothing seems to be happening."

The man smiled.

Steve took a sip of his tea and sighed, "The company founder is barely aware of me or, if he is, he's purposely ignoring me. When I shared the details of my lucrative deal at our last group meeting, all he could muster was, 'good job.'"

The man took a sip and pointed out the window. "Do you see that bamboo tree?"

Steve peered out to see a thick, tall clump of dark green bamboo, seven to eight inches in diameter, shooting straight up into the sky.

"That's the Chinese bamboo."

Steve nodded, wondering secretly why this man seemed so obsessed with trees.

"When you plant the Chinese bamboo, for the first four years, you don't see any visible growth. I mean, you keep fertilizing and watering it, but there seems to be no change—almost nothing above the soil, at best a small bud and some leaves."

Steve checked out the tree again. It was difficult to imagine that towering bamboo as a small bud.

"And you begin to wonder," the man continued. "Is the seed not good enough? Have your efforts all gone to waste? But then, in the fifth year, something magical happens. The bamboo grows a whopping 80 feet in just six weeks!"

"Incredible!" Steve took another glance at the bamboo tree, this time with newfound respect.

"So, keep watering your tree. And one day, you might look up to see a forest in its place."

"And what if nothing happens? What if my seed is a dud? Maybe I need to have a plan B."

"You can. But don't start fertilizing your backup plan to

rival plan A."

"What do you mean?"

"A backup plan is just that—a backup. So, once you've made it, forget about it till the need for it arises. But when you always have one eye on your backup, you will miss all that's happening right in front of you. With only one foot in the door, you will never allow yourself to give 100 percent to the task at hand.

"When I establish a goal, I don't think of backups. In my mind, my plan A is already a done deal," the man said, heading back into the kitchen.

"So, what is it that you do? I don't even know your name," Steve called out.

"What will you do with my name? Let it go. Let's spend the few hours we have in good conversation. That is enough, is it not?" the man answered from the kitchen, tinkering with pots and pans. Slowly, the warm buttery aroma of the homemade soup, spiced with ginger and celery and some other heady fragrances, floated into the room.

"But I have to call you by some name," Steve said, confounded.

The man came out, this time bearing two steaming bowls and a plate heaped with plump mulberries. "Call me Apricot Man, then. And about what I do, all I can say for now is that I am working on some ideas for my next project."

"Now," he said, placing the bowl in front of Steve, "why don't you have this soup and tell me how it is. This is *thukpa*, a local Tibetan vegetable soup. And these mulberries are compliments of our garden tree."

Steve took a big spoonful of the liquid goodness, filling his mouth with a symphony of flavor. For a moment, he was speechless. He leaned his head back and watched the bamboo trees rustling in the wind. A small bird, perched atop the gate, jabbed at a tiny berry in its front claw while the clouds drifted aimlessly in the skies. The whole of existence seemed to be in repose. But then, the vision of Susan closing his deal came scurrying back into his mind!

"So, how do you deal with failures? What's the mantra you live by?" Steve asked, gulping down another spoon of goodness.

"What is failure? A result you don't like. If the result falls in line with your expectation, you automatically label it a success. But remember, on its own, a result is just an event, an outcome. So don't get stuck in categorizing your life experiences as successes or failures. Instead, treat them as stepping stones to your end goal. Learn from them ... both the good and the bad. Don't let any experience go to waste. And once you commit to a goal, remain focused on it. Don't allow the fear of any other result dilute your focus," the man answered, resting his bowl on the table.

"And what if you do fail—I mean ... get a different result? The fear of consequences is always there," Steve asked.

"No problem. Reverse it."

"How?"

"As I said, view it as a new opportunity for growth, a possibility for learning something powerful and life-transforming. If you look back at your life, you will see that it is your failures that have taught you your most valuable lessons. Success often has the opposite effect—it makes you complacent, rigid. So, the next time you get a result you don't like, view it as an opportunity!"

"Don't you ever get tired of all this positivity?"

"Tell me, if you had a choice to live life with joy or suffering, what would you choose?" the man asked.

"Joy, of course. But suffering claws its way in. You cannot avoid pain."

"Pain and suffering are not the same," said the man. "Pain is necessary. It's a signal that we need to pay attention to something or that something is not right. Pain, like any other feeling, is a temporary state. And it should be treated as such. Learn from it. But never become attached to it. That's how you transform pain into suffering. To suffer is a choice you make. It arises when you become too attached to the grief, to the pain."

Steve nodded. He didn't have any trouble finding examples of this in his own life. In his twenties, after his first two serious relationships ended, he had concluded that either true love did not exist or, at the very least, that he wasn't worthy of it. And for a while, he carried his pain like armor, refusing to trust or let people in just to avoid rejection. But with time, those feelings dwindled, and he eventually fell in love with and married Christina. And even though the marriage did not stand the test of time, the relationship had not been a complete loss. They had their moments and, in many ways, Christina's presence had helped him come face-to-face with parts of his personality he had not seen or refused to see until then. For example, his constant need to be right, no matter what, or his obsession with his status in life.

Wow! Steve realized that this was the first time since the divorce he had seen his marriage as more than an abject failure. He was healing … a little.

"Your pain becomes so much a part of you that you start wearing it like a badge," the man said, bringing Steve back to the present.

Steve agreed. "Yes, and sometimes like armor."

"Yes, very right. And once you get attached to your pain, you have committed yourself to prolonged misery. But when you can see every event as an opportunity to experience life, there are no failures or successes … only more possibilities."

"That makes perfect sense right now," said Steve. "But, in moments of deep pain, it's difficult to truly embrace such wisdom, especially when you've given your all to a task or situation."

"What do you have faith in?" asked the man, unexpectedly.

"Excuse me?" Steve replied, confused.

"You must have faith in something, someone, some idea?"

"Frankly, the way the world is moving, I don't have much faith in anything. But yes ... I have faith in myself."

"Fantastic. That is enough. If you have faith in yourself, it means you have faith in life."

"Are they the same? Having faith in yourself and having faith in life?" Steve asked, trying to connect the dots.

"Of course! You are a part of life, so how can your experiences be separated from it? It's only the human ego that creates and revels in this separation. Even the whole argument around 'man versus nature' is wrong and has led us to the current environmental crisis. How can you be 'versus' something that you are part of?"

Steve nodded. He couldn't help but be in complete agreement with the "man versus nature."

The man continued. "The solutions to your predicaments flow out of this very nature. It's like a part trying to defeat the whole. In doing so, it only defeats itself. Hence, never be an enemy to life; be its accomplice. If you have faith in yourself, then you have to have faith in life as well."

Steve folded his arms. The man made a lot of good points, but he still wasn't completely convinced by the faith debate.

"OK, let's set aside the question of faith. Look at the world around you; we have close to nine million species on this one planet," the man noted. "And this planet is just one piece of rock in an entire solar system, and this solar system is just one speck in a vast galaxy, and so on. And everything is orderly, right? The sun comes out every day; bees pollinate, birds sing, children are born, trees grow, the wheat ripens in the field, and a star explodes in a distant galaxy. Everything seems to simultaneously be working symbiotically, in chaos, and in harmony ... an organized chaos! Doesn't that make you wonder if there is more to life than just coincidence? A higher intelligence at play, perhaps?"

"Oh, don't tell me you believe in miracles and stuff," Steve scoffed.

"Of course, I believe in miracles. They are happening every day, all around you. Inside of you, as well ... literally as we speak. Do you know your blood has the same concentration of salt as the ocean? Or that your bones are four times stronger than concrete? Or that your heart beats about 100,000 times a day ... all silently and effortlessly, without any special instruction or interference from you? Isn't this all a miracle? And if all this is happening without YOUR participation to keep YOU alive, doesn't that make you think there might be a bigger plan at work?"

Steve laughed self-consciously. "I don't know."

"Good ... 'I don't know' is a better answer. That at least opens the possibility to know. So, tell me, have you always been fighting life? Or is it a recent occurrence?"

Steve laughed and deliberately waved the question off. But deep down ... something quivered, a small doubt that bloomed into a larger existential question. *Had* he always been fighting life?

A moment of silence presented itself, and Steve internally acknowledged that it would be difficult to leave the company of the Apricot Man. The man did not mince words, yet his speech was never judgemental. And best of all, with him,

Steve could suddenly connect the little and big things in life. It was as if every leaf, branch, pebble, and mountain had some higher purpose, some transcendent meaning.

One thing this journey had done, Steve admitted, was that it brought alive the magic of unbridled conversation. Conversation unencumbered by an agenda or motive—the kind he never had back home. The pure joy of discussing an idea, sharing an experience, exploring the boundaries of a belief was something that had been missing from his interactions for some time now.

Given that he always had limited time (or so he thought), he conversed with people only when he wanted to highlight his achievements or gain something. Often, he simply waited for the other person to finish talking so he could talk again. His ex-wife had always complained he was too mercenary in his dealings. And today, he realized that she might be right.

He wanted to talk more, but it was time to meet the woman who was coming to give him a piece of his life back: his credit cards and money. So, he said goodbye and extended his thanks to the Apricot man for all he had shared.

Significance:
A for *Attraction*

> *"When you want something, all the universe conspires in helping you to achieve it."*
>
> —Paulo Coelho

In this chapter, cosmic forces conspired to help Steve meet the Apricot Man. This serendipitous interaction highlights the A in SPARK—the power of Attraction, which aligns to the Universal law that supports that what you seek is also seeking you.

Let's analyze some additional ideas around the concept of Attraction:

Use your focus and attention to breed Attraction.

We all invariably invite what our attention is focused on. As Rumi said, "What you seek is seeking you." For example, couples expecting a baby will notice more pregnant couples than they did before. In the same vein, when our minds are fixated on a particular goal, we are naturally more in tune with people, information and activities related to it.

You are a "living magnet" who has the power to attract people, ideas and opportunities into your life. Your dominant thoughts act as the pull and push of these magnetic fields; whether they are positive or negative, your focused thoughts accordingly attract their consequences.

Brian Tracy, who co-wrote the book *What You Seek is Seeking You* with me, explains that our brains have evolved to include a reticular cortex, which is responsible for motor control, sensory control, visceral control and control of consciousness. Much like an old-school telephone switchboard in a large office building used to direct calls, your reticular cortex contains an activating system that naturally manages messages like goals, objectives, plans and dreams. It is through the reticular cortex that you are made intensely aware and highly alert to other humans and societal events in your environment. This awareness helps you achieve your ambitions. However, without clear goals and focused thoughts, you are unable to optimize the power of this function.

Turn to your belief to access the "Soul of the World."

In the international bestselling book, *The Alchemist,* Paulo Coelho describes the interconnectedness between living and non-living things as a divine connection or "Soul of the World." According to the book, you are closest to the Soul of the World when you want something with all your heart. There is a volume of scientific evidence that shows how our thoughts have immediate and tangible effects on ourselves and the environment around us.

Many people see the world as a threatening place and, because they do, the world turns out to be just that. But when we truly believe that the Universe is conspiring for us, not against us, and that forces cooperate through us, not around us, we are able to access the Soul of the World and attract positive energy into our lives.

Harness the power of intention and desire.

Deepak Chopra's *Seven Spiritual Laws of Success* explores the power of intention and desire. In it, he shares, "Inherent in every desire are the mechanics for its fulfillment." Just as our mind has the power to energize our body to speak particular words, lift our arm or write with a pen, it can also exercise these intentions beyond our physical realm, in the field of pure consciousness, where our intentions can manifest through Universal forces.

One of the founding fathers of quantum physics, Nobel Prize winner Max Planck, once said that the "Mind is the matrix of all matter." This infinite and intelligent mind is the entity that our ancestors referred to as "infinite consciousness." It is believed that we, being part of the infinite and powerful consciousness, have the innate ability to influence matter and fulfill our desires.

Create crystal clear goals.

Research has shown that increased motivation, self-esteem, self-confidence and autonomy are just a few of the valuable benefits we gain from setting crystal clear goals. Clear goals, set with some form of higher purpose, result in higher success rates than vague or nebulous goals because they attract self-reinforcing behavior, both from the outside world and from our own internal system.

One way to internalize your crystal-clear goals is to visualize the success you seek. To do so, you want to make this visualization of success a daily part of your active imagination. This practice touches on the fundamental premise of the law of attraction—you attract what you are focused on.

Practice "Active Hope."

While it seems like a simple concept, hope is a critical driver of transformational change in your life. Hope should never be passive but boldly asserted in your subconscious and conscious endeavors.

"Active hope" has three key ingredients:

Desire: Active hope relies on a consistent, clear, and burning desire. Vague desires or desires that keep changing are fleeting, while a burning desire persists. If you are missing a burning desire, make it your burning desire to find out what your burning desire is.

Effort: Active hope requires persistent and focused effort. Hope without effort, focus and persistence can lead to a feeling of powerlessness. In contrast, focused and persistent effort leads to a greater feeling of agency and responsibility for your circumstances and optimism about your destiny.

Faith: Active hope requires a sense of faith in a higher power to do the right thing for you once you have done your part.

Active hope combines clarity of our intentions with agency over our circumstances and belief in forces beyond our control to cultivate greater optimism and attract positive forces in our lives.

Set Big Hairy Audacious Goals.

Michelangelo once said, "The greater danger for most of us lies not in setting our aim too high and falling short, but in setting our aim too low and achieving our mark."

In their book, *Built to Last: Successful Habits of Visionary Companies,* Jim Collins and Jerry Porras coined the term "Big Hairy Audacious Goals" or BHAGs. These are visionary, long-term, ambitious goals. According to Collins and Porras, setting these kinds of goals can be inspiring for the company's employees, leadership and investors alike. Similarly, such goals can be motivating for individuals, too. The more audacious you are with goal setting, the more audacity you invite into your life to achieve them.

One day, I was coaching my son in soccer, and I asked him to increase his practice time on a critical assisting pass into the penalty box for a teammate to score a goal with a header. Unfortunately, every time he crossed the ball to me, it would end up falling at chest height—which is not ideal because scoring with the chest is difficult. The next day, during a practice session where his actual coach was instructing the team to execute a similar drill, the coach instructed them to aim for the top of a baseball fence that stood behind the goal. I honestly expected the drill to be a disaster because my son had been struggling to pass the ball at head level, which was ten times lower than the baseball fence. To my astonishment, he hit the mark not once, not twice, but three times! Finally, the difference became clear to me: the coach set a big hairy audacious goal to aim higher, and in doing so, he helped my son reach it.

A life lesson to take away: do the same with your ambitions.

Tap into the Universe with larger-than-self aspirations.

While aspiration and ambition for personal gain can be motivating, be aware of greed lurking in the guise of ambition. Greed is like a bottomless pit; no matter how much of it you fill, it will always remain empty. Aspirations grounded in selfishness, greed, or competitiveness are not aligned with the natural flow of the Universe, which is rooted in giving and taking. When you set aspirations that are larger than self, ones that benefit society and the environment around you, you tap into the power of the Universe and attract circumstances that support and foster your goals.

Stay detached from the outcome.

Healthy aspirations require a balance between ambition and attachment. It is important to set clear and consistent goals to manifest your intentions and desires into the Universe. However, it is also important not to become too attached to the intended outcome of your aspirations.

Detachment is a central concept in Zen Buddhist philosophy. One of the most important technical terms for detachment in Buddhist philosophy is "wú niàn," which literally means "no thought." This does not signify the literal absence of thought but the state of being "unstained" (bù rán) by thought.

The Bhagavad Gita is also wonderfully explicit on this point. Krishna tells Arjuna that acting with detachment means doing the right thing for its own sake because it needs to be done without worrying about success or failure. Detachment is rarely something we achieve once and for all. It is the moment-by-moment, day-by-day process of accepting reality as it presents itself; by doing our best to align our actions with what we think is right and surrendering attachment to the outcome.

Detachment does not mean not caring. It is about doing your best and leaving the rest. Detachment from the outcome allows you to feel the benefits of the journey of transformation rather than just focusing on the anticipated outcome. Living in an unpredictable world means that success may never be exactly as you envision it. However, if you have faith in the Universal powers around you, you will see that the success you achieve will exceed your expectations because it was curated by the Universe. You will come to realize that success and happiness are in the journey and not the outcome.

A renowned Sufi saint once remarked, "Detachment is not that you should own nothing, but rather that nothing should own you."

Having crystal clarity around your goals, taking daily action towards realizing these aspirations, setting intentions that manifest into the Universe and cultivating a sense of detachment from the outcome will allow you to attract success, significance and happiness into your life.

REFLECTION QUESTIONS:

- What are your aspirations in life? Are they crystal clear or vague? Are they big hairy audacious goals? Are they self-serving or larger-than-self?

- What kind of thoughts are part of your self-talk? Do they reflect alignment and belief in your goals?

- Have you noticed any accidents, coincidences or setbacks in your life that could serve as a Universal sign? What do you think the Universe is trying to tell you?

- Have you ever set a goal and been disappointed? What was the driver for your disappointment? Were you attached to a specific idea of what success looks like? What happened instead, and how did it serve your lifelong learning?

HOW TO GET STARTED:

- Clearly define your inspiring and energizing goals.

  _____
  _____
  _____

- Start manifesting your aspirations into the Universe. You can do this in the following ways:

  - **Visualization:** As soon as you wake up, spend the next three waking minutes imagining and feeling what your "best day ever" will look like.

  - **Vision boarding:** Learn how to create visuals to communicate the ideas and stories you want to materialize. This can impact all the right emotions that drive your daily effort.

  - **Affirmations:** An affirmation, like a mantra, is a powerful statement you can repeat to yourself daily to describe the goal you are aiming for.

  - **Imagination:** Forming mental images or concepts of what you wish to create is a powerful internalization tool. Through imagination, you can transport yourself beyond the limits of your conscious mind to tap into the reserves of the subconscious.

- List a few ways you might start manifesting your aspirations.

  _____
  _____
  _____
  _____

- Start noticing and recording accidents, coincidences and setbacks in your life. Think about how these could serve as universal signs to guide you towards success. Imagine the entire Universe conspiring to help you achieve your goals.

  _____
  _____
  _____
  _____

PART 4

Story:
Peak Performance

As Steve scrambled down the hill, back to the main road, rain fell softly. The smell of the forest rose thick in the wind that coursed down slopes majestically resting all around this north Indian hill station.

For a moment, Steve stopped and looked up at the great pine trees, at the raindrops slithering down the needles into the sodden earth. It was a passing shower, and the sun would soon beam out, shafting through the branches, turning the dancing leaves, the tarred roads, the metal balustrades of the boundary wall into gleaming ornaments.

People, bundled up in jackets and coats, sweaters and bright scarves, scurried up and down the road. A small herd of cows sat silently in the middle, quietly ruminating over the approaching dusk. Steve rubbed his hands and arms, shivering slightly in the evening chill. To get the blood flowing, he sprinted down the slope, his pace quickening with the incline.

The cafe suddenly floated into view like a glow worm around the turn, a solitary glass-walled building perched on the outcropping of a cliff. A row of pots bursting with bright green ferns hung from the rafters. Through the tall windows, he could see a large hall filled with a smattering of chairs, sofas and small diamond-shaped yellow lamps hanging from the ceiling.

A fire crackled in the hearth at one end, and a shelf filled with books lined the other wall. People stood near the balcony overlooking the valley below—a few were alone with their books, some couples were whispering and laughing, and a small group gathered around a sofa. The strains of a guitar streamed out as soon as Steve pushed open the heavy door.

Steve scoped out a table with a valley view and walked past the group gathered around the guitar player, a woman sitting with folded legs on a chair, playing softly, her eyes shut.

He checked the time on his new mobile to make sure he wasn't running late. In fact, he was early. He aimed the camera on his tiny phone at the view of the mountains surrounding the dark valley. Half a moon dangled over the canopy of a tree, and a thin curling column of smoke drifted from a white house perched on a hill.

"You will get a better angle from that table."

He turned to see a woman standing behind his chair, pointing towards the table on his left. It was the guitar player, he realized with a sudden thrill.

"Hi, I am Nadia. You must be Steve?"

"How did you …?"

"You are the only one here with the weight of a torrid journey on his face," the woman smiled.

Dressed in a white tee with olive green cargos and brown hiking shoes, carrying a jammed hiking pack over one shoulder, she was of medium build, strong and wiry, with veins standing out on her bare arms. She had modest features, with a square jaw and a small, upturned nose that crinkled when she smiled. But it was her eyes, widely spaced and luminous, that lent her face a quality of eternal delight. Her hair was knotted on the top of her head, with a few tendrils escaping and hovering around her face, glittering in hues of coffee, honey, and amber in the light of the fire crackling behind her.

"Sorry about delaying this meeting. There was a landslide on the way, and our bus had to wait till they cleared the rubble."

"No problem! These landslides seem pretty prevalent during the rains, especially around these hilly parts," Steve said, accepting her apology.

"You're right—every time the heavens open to nourish the earth, it can get ugly around these parts. And with the increasing deforestation and encroachment, the frequency of landslides has unfortunately increased."

"I hope no one was hurt," he said, motioning for her to take a seat.

"Everyone is safe. But first," she said, quickly releasing the strap to remove her hiking bag. She swung it around, dug into it, and pulled out a smaller knapsack.

"This is your package … your renewed license back into civilization," she grinned.

Steve accepted the bag, laughing, as she finally took her seat.

"The bag should contain an iPhone, a credit card, 70,000 rupees cash in an envelope and some clothes. Your office is already working on the passport, and they will courier it to the local post office in the next few days."

"Thank you. But you can keep the phone. I already have one, and it's doing its job pretty well," he said bashfully.

"Oh, I think you should keep it. Your office has already called three times to make sure I am on schedule to meet with you. So, you, my dear sir, are very important, and they will not like it if I were to take it back," she said, her eyes twinkling with mischievous amusement.

Steve laughed self-consciously. "Thank you for taking the time to deliver this to me! And thanks to the India office for arranging everything so soon. So do you work in our Delhi office?"

"No, I work independently. I'm a travel writer. Your company contacted their travel agency in Canada to inquire if they had anyone on this side of the world that could help. They in turn reached out to me to see if I could meet you. I had previously worked with them on a few projects, and I had kept in touch, so luckily, they knew I was traveling in this region."

"Interesting. Listen, if you are not in a rush, will you join me for a coffee and a croissant, perhaps?" Steve proposed with a tinge of nervousness. "It's been three days since I have had some extra money in my pocket, and I have this internal urge to celebrate. And I would love to have some company, too."

The woman checked her watch. "Coffee sounds good. And may I suggest the almond muffins? They are way better. And, oh yes, I'll have the club sandwich, too."

"Sure ... anything else?" Steve asked, amused and impressed at how confident she was.

"No, that should be good for now," she said, her face completely straight.

"So, are you writing a travel story while you are here?" Steve said, motioning at the waiter who was hovering close by.

"Yes, a couple, and I'm also working on my book now. And you ... what is it that you do?" Nadia asked as the waiter came over, quickly taking their order.

"Well, I graduated with a corporate law degree from Harvard. Then, straight into some traditional apprentice positions with some pro bono work. Slowly worked my way up, and today, I handle mergers and acquisitions for large companies across North America," Steve replied casually, slightly pausing at the end.

"How large?" asked Nadia.

"It varies. But I can safely say I don't manage transactions below $90 million."

Nadia let out a low, prolonged whistle of surprise.

"Bye, Nadia," someone shouted from the door. Steve turned around and recognized one of the young men who sat in her group by the sofa.

She smiled and waved back.

"I'll email you the project by this evening," the man added.

Nadia gave him thumbs up.

"Are they your colleagues?" Steve asked with dampened curiosity.

"Students, actually," she replied.

"So, you are also a teacher. What do you teach?"

"Mountain climbing. I moonlight as an instructor at the Regional Mountaineering Centre here in McLeod Ganj. It was our last class this past weekend. We were on our way back from the campsite when the agency called about you."

"Mountain climbing ... Wow! What's the highest peak you've climbed?" Steve asked, impressed but also a little nervous, simply imagining being up that high.

"Oh ... Everest," Nadia replied casually as the waiter delivered their food. She took a bite of her muffin.

Steve, about to sip on his coffee, stopped his cup midway to glance at her. He then threw his head back in laughter, as if he thought she was joking.

Nadia continued eating the muffin, unfazed by his disbelief.

"Wait ... are you serious?" Steve said.

"Why do you find it so hard to believe that I climbed Everest?" she wondered, her mouth full.

"Oh no, of course, I believe it. I just never met anyone who scaled the world's highest peak and then nonchalantly slipped it in the conversation while chewing on a muffin. That's incredible! So, tell me ... how was it, standing on top of the world? How did you feel?"

"Humbled ... grateful ... speechless ... and that doesn't even begin to describe it. I still can't think of words to express what I felt."

"When did you do this?"

"Two years ago."

"It must have taken a great deal of training and preparation?"

"Yup. There is no other option. The mountain demands it. You have to be in top physical, emotional and psychological condition."

"How tall is Mount Everest again?"

"29,035 feet."

"Phew ..." Steve said, leaning forward on the table, his heart beating a little bit faster at the number. "How long did you train?"

"The first time, it took me a year to get into Everest shape. The next two times, the training periods were shorter because my body had already acclimatized, but the sessions themselves were way more intense."

"Hold on—you tried *three times*?!" Steve could believe she climbed Everest once ... but three times?

"The first time, they had to cancel the climb due to bad weather conditions. The second time, I tore cartilage in my ankle and nearly lost two of my toes to severe frostbite, so I had to return midway through my ascent."

"Oh man, you must have been very upset."

"Heartbroken! To come so close and having to turn back was a real bummer," Nadia said, pursing her lips.

Suddenly, Steve remembered the Burton deal. He hadn't thought of it in hours.

"But after brooding for a month, I got bored of feeling sorry for myself," Nadia continued. "How long can you keep lamenting the same thing? Then, I thought to myself, there is only one area where I have full control: my state of mind. No individual or event should influence me, in any way, positive or negative, unless I permit it. And on my terms. How I choose to frame my experiences is entirely my decision."

"Seriously? Didn't you, like, for one moment doubt that you may be deluding or fooling yourself?"

"When you have a choice between adopting a path that empowers you and one that breaks you down, what would you choose?" she asked.

Steve suddenly remembered Apricot Man's concept of reversing your fear. "I guess that's one way to look at it," he said.

"Well, it worked, didn't it? I did conquer that mountain in the end," she shrugged with a hint of pride.

"Yes ... but you can only say it was successful in hindsight. Question is, what kept you going before you stepped back on Everest soil?"

"Each time the mountain sent me back, I trained harder, better. Became stronger, mentally and physically."

"Ah, like the adage, that which does not kill us makes us stronger ... right?"

"Yup, something like that," she said, unapologetically swiping a slice of his club sandwich from his plate.

He couldn't help but smile ear-to-ear. He had never seen a woman eat so much without a drop of remorse. It was refreshing!

"What ... you find it funny?" Nadia said with a glare.

"Oh no, not at all! But it is the second time today that

I've heard someone talking about trusting life. And it has got me questioning my own terms with it. Anyway, back to you. You must have been a little worried ... what if the third time was also ...?"

"Of course. There was self-doubt ... and a great deal of fear. On the mountain, everything is temporary and unpredictable. One moment you are climbing up, and the very next, hanging upside down. But then, life can also be that topsy-turvy. Over time, you learn to trust yourself. You know that in the end, you will find your way back to doing what you're passionate about.

"Instead of becoming paranoid that I might not make it up the mountain for the third time, I shifted that negative energy to pursuing new possibilities and encounters in the time and space life had suddenly afforded me. By being comfortable with this position and fully accepting it, I ended up finding a major sponsor in the process."

"How did that happen?" asked Steve.

"Through my climbing contacts, I was invited to speak about my Everest experiences at an adventure sports seminar. They wanted to hear about the learning from the two failed attempts. Someone in the audience happened to be a sales rep for an adventure gear company. He told his company about me. When they learned that I was also a popular blogger, they offered to sponsor my next climb to promote their gear. So, everything worked out in the end."

"That's an amazing story! You must chronicle your experiences."

"What do you think my book is about?" she grinned, finally wiping her mouth and hands with a napkin and settling back in her seat.

"So, tell me about this preparation. What did it entail?

"First, you have to acclimate your body to live with

extremely cold temperatures at extreme altitudes. That entails a strict physical regime. Then, there are the basic mountaineering skills, like learning to rappel with your pack on, improving your cramponing technique—both on and off rock, and on ice and snow. Plus, you must learn to use ascenders and jumars on a fixed-line and develop your overall high altitude living abilities. And finally, you must practice, practice and practice! At least a few times on slopes above 10,000 feet with your gear and equipment, this alone can weigh around 50–60 pounds. Your cardiovascular system, your strength endurance, tolerance ... your whole system needs to function at peak condition."

"Sounds pretty tough!"

"It is! But if you are not tough, the mountain will eat you up and spit you out. It's also more than your physical stamina; you need to build your mental and emotional endurance because, as I said, mountain conditions change unexpectedly and horribly."

"Yes ... well, not that I know from personal experience. But I watched the movie *Cliffhanger* as a child. You know the one with Sylvester Stallone?" Steve said.

"Oh yes, I have seen that one," she replied, her eyes wide open.

"It made a real impression on me. The woman, falling off the zip line into the abyss ... Now, that single-handedly turned me off rock climbing for good. Not that I'd ever tried it or had any desire to. But it's crazy how you make one mistake, and there's no coming back! And some of those altitude scenes made me realize I have a fear of heights," Steve snorted.

"It's true; it can get scary. I can vividly picture being stuck inside my tent, the plastic contraption flapping like a paper bag, and the wind howling outside, threatening to hurl me off the mountain, my throat parched, thermos empty, and my two feet feeling like two bags of lead strapped to my legs. You can't help but think about death in those moments ... a lot! But then, those moments also make you feel the most alive. That's the paradox of life, I guess."

"I agree ... I had this experience not so long ago ..." Steve mumbled under his breath as he looked away.

Nadia caught what he said, "Oh yes, the car mugging. I heard they had a gun?"

"Yes ... but let's not talk about that. Let's continue talking about your training. How did you even know where to begin ...?"

"Baby steps. Every step brings you closer," she continued.

"What did you do?" asked Steve.

"I started by making a few changes to my lifestyle. Then those changes led to more changes. Like an upside-down pyramid, one habit led to two more, and so on. Whether it was my diet and sleep, my exercise program at the gym, my daily runs, my climbing skills or finally the practice sessions at training camps—I ritualized every activity and strictly followed the schedule."

"You make it sound so simple."

"It is ... if you want it badly enough. Over time, I realized the real resistance comes less from the body and more from the mind. Our minds are primed for short-term gratification, so I started small. And in the beginning, I made it a point to reward myself for every mini-goal I achieved. Whether it was allowing myself to eat my favorite brownie after a long run, or a spa session after two weeks of intense training, I kept my mind from becoming grouchy and complaining about being deprived of things it liked. The key was to keep it engaged and motivated with little victories. And once the habit kicks in, you build momentum—things start getting easier. Bit by bit, your mind stops resisting and complaining. And once you begin to see the results, the activity itself becomes self-sustaining. And once your mind starts working with you, your body responds even faster. The body is, after all, programmed to support your mind."

"Seems like the training was long and grueling. There must have been days when you just wanted to sleep in, or binge on some fast food, or …"

"Yes, of course. There are many temptations. There were many times I just wanted to go out partying into the night with my friends, spend the weekend lounging in my PJs, permanently turn off my alarm instead of setting it for dawn. But, as I saw it, each choice I made could either take me closer or further away from my goal."

"Interesting. Have you heard of Kobe Bryant?" he asked.

"The basketball player who passed away recently. I have never seen him play, but I hear he was phenomenal."

"Yes, he was. And he was not just a phenomenal basketball player; he was an amazing human being. Truly, one of the most inspiring people of our generation. After a trying time in his life, he adopted an alter ego, naming himself the 'Black Mamba.' It was a name he used to separate his life on and off the court."

"Black Mamba?"

"Yeah, like the venomous snake. The moniker instilled in him that killer instinct, much like the animal that inspired the name. With it, he became exceedingly difficult to compete against. The Mamba brand ultimately became so popular that he later created the Mamba Sports Academy to provide training for competitors at all levels, in a variety of sports, to build that killer mentality."

"I see you are very fond of him."

"Yup … big fan! He also wrote a book called, *The Mamba*

Mentality: How I Play. You should check it out."

"I will," she said, glancing at her mobile.

Noticing this, he asked, "So what are you planning to do next?" He hoped she'd say "nothing," and they could continue their conversation.

"Next ... as in?" she asked, looking back at him.

"You have already scaled the world's highest peak. You are in the process of writing your book. So, what's next? Do you fear you may have hit a plateau?" Steve asked, continuing his probe.

"Is that question directed at me or yourself?" Nadia asked, laughing.

"Hmmm, I guess you're right. I'm indirectly asking myself, through you. To be honest, I have started feeling a little jaded. As if I have lost my spark. Nothing excites me very much anymore. It's like I have all these shiny toys, but I am done playing with them. Do you ever get that feeling?"

"Of course, I do. But if I have the freedom to be, I don't think there is any room for feeling bored for very long."

"Freedom to be what?"

"Well, for that answer, we will have to meet again. I'm getting very late for a dinner appointment I've committed to."

Steve smiled, his heart skipping a few beats. Partly in anticipation and partly due to anxiety.

"Circumstances do not make the man, they reveal him."

Significance:
R for *Resilience*

"*Circumstances do not make the man, they reveal him.*"

—James Allen

In this chapter, Nadia shared her story of how she overcame two failed attempts to conquer the tallest mountain in the world. This feat highlights the power of Resilience—a commitment to consistent good habits and a relentlessly positive attitude. This is the R in SPARK!

Let's investigate the concept of Resilience a little more below:

Maintain unwavering good habits.

The first step towards cultivating resilience in your life is to build a set of good habits you can rely on. Ones that are unwavering, be it good times or bad. Focusing on healthy routines can enhance your productivity when you are on a roll and give you a sense of stability when you are experiencing turmoil.

One idea is to practice the "Hour of Power," which includes 20 minutes of exercise, 20 minutes of meditation and 20 minutes of reading something uplifting every single day. If you do not feel like you have an hour to spare every day, aim to go to bed an hour earlier the night before and wake up one hour earlier in the morning. The last hour before bed is rarely productive or worth staying up for, whereas the first hour in the morning is the perfect opportunity to start your day in a way that supercharges your life. My friend Robin Sharma elaborates this point in detail in his wonderful book, *The 5 AM Club*.

If you practice consistent habits such as the "Hour of Power" daily, you will build the foundation for a healthy routine that will stick with you in good times and bad.

Become inverse paranoid.

W. Clement Stone was once described as "inverse paranoid." He believed the Universe was conspiring in his favor rather than colluding to do him harm. He looked for an opportunity in everything that happened, whether it was good, bad or neutral.

In simple terms, a paranoid person believes the world has the power to do them harm. So, an inverse paranoid individual believes the world is out there to enrich and empower him or her.

This attitude looks at every wound and sorrow as a blessing. Rumi gives this lovely example: "Realize that you are a rock, a diamond if you will. Every rub and friction you experience is therefore not something trying to destroy. It is trying to polish. Trying to better. Trying to smoothen the rough, to clear the unclear, to beautify, and to make you something that in the end is so elegant and magnificent that you are worth far beyond your weight in gold."

Aspire to Enlightened Persistence.

Persistence is the single most important predictor of success. What makes some people successful, and others not, usually lies in their choice to persevere.

Michael Jordan once said, "I've missed more than 9,000 shots in my career. I have lost 300 games. Twenty-six times, I have been trusted to take the game winning shot and missed. I have failed over and over and over again in my life. And that is why I succeeded."

When J. K. Rowling wrote the first *Harry Potter* novel, 12 different publishers rejected her book. Even Bloomsbury, the publishing house that finally purchased Rowling's manuscript, advised Rowling to "get a day job."

Walt Disney was turned down 302 times before he got the financing he needed to build Disney World.

Joe Biden became the president of the United States in 2020. Although he had previously served as the vice president, his life had been full of hardships. He lost his wife and his daughter in a road accident while going to purchase a Christmas tree. One of his sons died due to brain cancer. His second son was discharged from the US Navy due to cocaine addiction. He also suffered two brain aneurysms when he was a senator and spent his entire life coping with a severe stutter. Despite these challenging circumstances, he became the president of one of the most powerful countries in the world at the age of 77.

It is not surprising then that Thomas Edison once said, "Genius is one percent inspiration and 99 percent perspiration." While many of these individuals were born with great talents and skills, all of them, without exception, had to go through hardships and persevere to succeed.

Make failure an investment, not a hardship. Learn from every failure, and then apply this learning to your next attempt. Better yet, take the attitude that there are no failures in life, only lessons to learn from. Then, you will become an unstoppable force. Through these struggles, you will realize that it is not just what you achieve but what you become along the way. This will cultivate a growth mindset, which interprets challenge and failure not as a signal to throw in the towel but as a natural, healthy part of human growth and achievement.

Og Mandino said it beautifully: "I will be likened to the raindrop which washes away the mountain; the ant who devours a tiger; the star which brightens the earth; the slave who builds a pyramid. I will build my castle one brick at a time for I know that small attempts, repeated, will complete any undertaking. I will persist until I succeed."

Persistence is often the deciding factor between having a dream and living it. Enlightened persistence implies that your persistence is grounded in a clear life purpose that leverages your natural talents and serves the world around you. The combination of resilience and clarity of vision will propel you to achieve your goal.

Keep cultivating your Resilience, even when growth is not visible.

For the first four years of the Chinese bamboo tree's life, you cannot see any visible growth above the soil. However, in the fifth year, the bamboo grows to 80 feet in just six weeks. The example of the bamboo tree illustrates that growth occurs both above and below ground.

Similarly, we as individuals may be experiencing rapid internal growth that is not visible to the world. Our challenges and missteps may be teaching us lifelong lessons that will guide our future success, even though these may just appear to be failures. With a relentless focus on our noble aspirations and resilience to overcome our obstacles, we may suddenly experience transformational, visible growth at any time. However, if we stop nourishing our aspirations while we are still on the journey of internal growth, we will never know whether these goals could have been achieved.

The smallest of seeds may yield the mightiest of forests full of the grandest trees—from majestic redwoods to mighty oaks. By looking at the seed, it would be difficult to believe that a preeminent mix of roots, leaves, flowers and fruits is contained within it. We are also born from a small seed brimming with potential. But unless we become conscious of the magnificence within us and foster it, it may never actualize.

Much like the miracle of the Chinese bamboo tree, it can sometimes be difficult to assess what stage of growth we are in. Some of our low periods or failures may seem like an indication that we should give up; however, these might instead be periods of transformational growth that are building a strong foundation for long-term success. If you maintain faith in the idea that every life experience is an opportunity for growth, you will cultivate an unwavering resilience that fosters your eventual success.

Tear up your Plan B.

Jihae Shin, a researcher at the Wisconsin School of Business at the University of Wisconsin-Madison, and the Wharton

School at the University of Pennsylvania's Katherine L. Milkman performed a series of studies that examined how having a backup plan impacts success. One study group was offered rewards if they did well on a test at the first go-round. Researchers then told all other study groups that they'd have to create backup plans before taking the test, just in case they did not do well. The groups forced to develop backup plans ended up consistently performing worse on the tests than the group who were rewarded for doing well the first time. The researchers concluded the simple act of thinking through your backup plan could subconsciously reduce your ability to succeed with your initial goal.[1]

When you take the approach of jumping off the cliff backward, there is no going back to the cliff. This means your first and only aim is to land in the water alive so that you can successfully swim your way to your destiny. People who take this approach are fully committed, and their subconscious mind allows them to dedicate all their energy to plan A rather than dividing their attention between plan A and plan B.

This does not mean becoming irresponsible and disregarding your familial or financial responsibilities. It means nurturing a mental state while you are working towards your goal where success is the only option. If things do not turn out the way you expect, you can reassess your options. But during the relentless pursuit of your goal, there are no plan Bs.

---

[1] Shin, Jihae, and Katherine L. Milkman. "How Backup Plans Can Harm Goal Pursuit: The Unexpected Downside of Being Prepared for Failure." Organizational Behavior and Human Decision Processes 135 (2016): 1–9. https://doi.org/10.1016/j.obhdp.2016.04.003.

Develop a Mamba Mentality.

Kobe Bryant's Mamba Mentality is a symbol of his dedication to excellence and resilience—not only in basketball but also in life. The Mamba Mentality that propelled him to greatness consists of fearlessness, relentlessness, resilience, obsessiveness and being the best version of yourself. These five principles indicate the importance of perseverance in the pursuit of success. The theme behind many of these principles is to focus on your goal rather than on the obstacles in your way.

You do not have to be a Kobe Bryant to cultivate a Mamba Mentality. During a visit to Tajikistan, I was conducting interviews with top executives at one of my client organizations to better understand the company culture, values and challenges. While I was conducting my interviews, the CEO informed me that a janitor in his group had requested a meeting with me and asked if I would be willing to speak with her for a few minutes. Although I was surprised by the request, I obliged. With the help of an interpreter, she shared the following:

"I don't know who you are, but you are important since you are meeting all the important people in the organization. However, let me tell you who I am! I am the cleaner, the one who is the first to come to work every morning before anyone comes in. I make sure all the offices are spick-and-span. At lunchtime, I do not go home, but I make sure I do another clean-up so people can work well in the afternoon. I am the last to go home in the evening, and I ensure that all the offices are clean for the next morning. I am a single mom—my husband left me to marry a Russian woman and sends me nothing and does not keep in touch. I have three young kids at home to support. Please do not shut down the operations of this company; I need my job!"

She had concluded in her mind that I was there to evaluate a plant closure because she was aware they had gone through some hardship. I assured her that her job was secure, and I acknowledged her gumption and dedication. I share this because, while this janitor is no Kobe Bryant, she displayed her own Mamba Mentality. She was fearless in her desire to speak with me, relentless in her request to keep the plant open, resilient despite the uncertain circumstances, obsessive about her work and dedicated to being the best version of herself and as a janitor at this company. For her, doing whatever it took to save her job and her family was her primary goal, and she took the necessary steps required to actualize this. If a single mom and cleaner in Tajikistan can demonstrate the principles of the Mamba Mentality, so can each of us.

Turn sorrow and loss into growth and enlightenment.

When I was a young boy, my parents moved our family from one part of town to another. In this new neighborhood, I did not have any friends. One day, I saw a few kids playing soccer on a nearby field. You could see that they were just kicking the ball around, and it was not a serious competition. I asked if I could join in, and they agreed. However, after a few minutes, they realized that I did not know how to play, so they made fun of me and asked me to sit out and watch instead. As a young child trying to make new friends, I was hurt and embarrassed.

I felt low for many days. Eventually, my uncle found out what happened and asked me what I was going to do about it. He made me realize that sitting around and sulking was not going to help me. Instead, the heart-to-heart motivated me to wake up early every morning and practice on my own for an hour.

Not only did I learn how to play, but in the next ten years that followed, I captained a highly competitive team with those same boys and fell in love with the game. The hurtful childhood experience gave birth to one of my greatest passions in life. I won many trophies and traveled to many cities playing the beautiful game. More importantly, soccer has now become a bonding experience for my son and me. I was his first coach, and because of it, our relationship is stronger. It's a godsend that we now share the same love for this sport.

Rumi said, "The wound is where the light enters." When you feel hurt or discouraged in life, think about how you might reframe this experience into an opportunity for growth and enlightenment. Rather than avoiding pain and upset throughout your life, think about how you can use these emotions to fuel your passion and drive.

Practice daily gratitude.

Research has found that when we express gratitude, the brain releases a surge of dopamine, a neurotransmitter that plays an important role in many vital functions.[2]

This surge of dopamine gives you a natural high, increasing the experience and duration of positive emotions. In addition to increasing dopamine, gratitude has also been associated with increased serotonin production. Serotonin is often called "the happiness chemical" because it contributes to feelings of well-being, stabilizes our mood, and helps us

---

[2] Chowdhury, Madhuleena Roy. "The Neuroscience of Gratitude and How It Affects Anxiety & Grief." PositivePsychology.com, January 7, 2022. https://positivepsychology.com/neuroscience-of-gratitude/.

feel more relaxed.

Practicing daily gratitude is an excellent way to foster resilience. Not only does it influence our brain to produce mood-enhancing hormones, but it also focuses our attention on the positive aspects of our life. Whether we are grateful for our positive experiences, our talents and skills, our support network and community or even our challenges and failures that have taught us something, gratitude allows us to see the good in all of life.

REFLECTION QUESTIONS:

- What are some of the positive habits you have in your life? How do they help your success? Do you practice them regularly, in good times and bad? Can you develop any further good habits that can boost your resilience?

- What would you consider to be the biggest failure of your life? How did you recover from it, and what did you learn in the process?

- What are you most grateful for in this life? Which of your positive experiences have been the most transformative? Which skills and talents are you most proud of? Who are your most avid supporters and cheerleaders?

- What challenges have been life-changing and helped you grow?

HOW TO GET STARTED:

- Begin your days, over the next work week, by practicing the "Hour of Power": 1) Exercise for 20 minutes 2) Meditate for 20 minutes, and 3) Read something uplifting for 20 minutes. Journal how you feel, as well as the effects it has on your day-to-day life.

  _____
  _____
  _____

- Practice inverse paranoia by writing a list of your biggest fears and worries, and then invert them. Think about how the Universe might conspire in your favor rather than against you. Visualize this positive outcome until you believe it.

  _____
  _____
  _____

- Start a gratitude journal. You can leverage a service such as the "5 Minute Journal" to start a daily gratitude practice.

  _____
  _____
  _____

PART 5

Story:
A Bridge to Know Where!

Steve checked into the best hotel in Dharamsala. And boy was he glad. Every small service, utility and luxury he took in was magnified a hundred times over. The clean scent of freshly laundered sheets, the tang of jasmine and neroli soaps in the washroom, the soft cushiony pair of handwoven bathroom slippers, the mint eclairs on his pillow, the delectable room service, the strains of Mozart in the lobby, the neat rectangles of the TV remote placed within arms-length of his bed … everything had acquired a special grace overnight. But one thing he missed was the company of new friends, the guileless smiles of people who had shared their meager meals with him. He realized that no amount of freshly baked bread from the hotel bakery could compete with that wholesome, yeasty aroma of that bun dipped into hot, ginger-spiced tea. And he was grateful he had the opportunity to enjoy both.

After taking a long leisurely bath, he swaddled himself in the long white bathrobe, poured himself a drink, and settled on the bed to check his recent emails on the new phone Nadia brought him. Good thing she forced him to hold on to it, too. One email was from Michelle, informing him that the final Burton meeting was delayed for a week due to an impromptu event hosted at the client's end. She also wanted to know when he hoped to depart so that she could organize the tickets for him to arrive in time for the rescheduled meeting.

He wrote back, letting her know he'd figure out his final plans after meeting Theo.

He called room service and ordered a big meal. Then, after settling some other work emails, he slipped under the covers and switched on the 7th episode of *Norsemen* on Netflix. But his attention kept wavering back to the Norsewoman he had met just a few hours ago. Nadia. Would he ever see her again? The thought made Steve restless.

Steve rang up Theo's number. But it was still unreachable.

That was just the excuse he needed! He immediately called Nadia to tell her how he had not been able to connect with Theo.

"Hmmm ... sometimes the low-hanging dense fog clouds can scatter cell signals. But don't worry, I'll try passing on the message if I meet someone from his village on my way out tomorrow."

"Oh, you will be passing by his village. Why didn't you tell me?"

"Not exactly *by* his village. Only halfway. But the route I take is through the hills, which are quite steep and tiring but reduce the arrival time. Besides, I didn't think you would be interested in where I was traveling to next or the deets about the route," she said in jest.

"But I am ... very much!" Steve exclaimed suddenly.

A deafening silence grew from the other end.

"I mean, in the route," he fumbled. "The sooner I get there, the better."

"Well then, I'll see you at 7 a.m. sharp outside the cafe where we met. Please be on time because I can't afford to be late for my meeting."

"Great … looking forward to it," Steve replied, unable to stop grinning as he hit the hay.

The next morning, they took a road that passed through a village and then over a small hill. She scaled, skipped, glided and leaped over rocks like a wild alpine antelope in full flight. Steve took her lead and did his best to keep up, silently thanking his lucky stars for the squash he played daily.

He finally found the breath to say, "You were talking about freedom yesterday," as they followed the path over a small stream that appeared suddenly behind a large mossy trunk.

"Yes … what about that?" she answered, hopping over the stream.

"Freedom to be what?" Steve asked.

"Freedom to be anything you choose—to grow in any direction—to transform yourself! No other life on this planet enjoys this type of independence and privilege; only humans do. And yet we complain about feeling shackled by life events or being bored in our current circumstances."

"It's not that easy," Steve reasoned. "Over time, we get settled in certain belief systems and patterns and habits."

"What's the point of clinging to beliefs and patterns if they do not serve us in our pursuit to be our most authentic selves? Nothing can be more tragic than expending this one precious life in apathy, complacency and self-loathing, especially when there's so much to experience."

"But certain life-affecting circumstances are not in our control," Steve argued.

"I agree. Certain things you cannot change. Like the family you are born into, your genetic makeup, the social milieu around you, and the externally influenced situations you can't help but encounter. But at the same time, you also have something ever-changing, fluid, something uniquely indeterminable in you … for example, your choice of response. Your free will!"

"Yes, but isn't free will also just a conditioned habit we have developed in response to certain recurring or life-changing experiences?"

"Yes … but if you are aware of this conditioning, you can step out of it."

"How?"

"Once you know of a better way, why would you use the old one? Tell me, why would you continue banging your head into the wall when you can see the door?" Nadia said, hiking up her pack. "Your conditioned response or memory is only good so far as it serves as a reference point for learning from your experience. But it should never become a trap. It shouldn't confine you to a pattern of counterproductive reactions or compulsions."

"Hmm … reminds me of my smoking days in high school," Steve remembered. "In the beginning, I did it just to fit in with my buddies. Then I used smoking as a stress buster during exams because I was very confident that I could drop the habit whenever I wanted. But it turned out that anytime I went on to face some form of stress or tension, my first instinct was to light up a cigarette. And by the time I was 23, I was smoking three packs a day. It took a severe bout of bronchitis and a year of chewing yucky nicotine gum to break me out of that habit."

"Any compulsion, good or bad, creates an imbalance. When a habit starts driving you instead of you driving it, it becomes a compulsion. And compulsions have a sneaky way of creeping up on you. In my case, it was an obsession with exercising ... I was working out three to four hours a day and on a restrictive diet. I lost so much body fat that I stopped ovulating. That was my warning bell! Instead of getting stronger, I was weakening my body. But later, when I was training for the climb, I was always mindful of maintaining a balance."

"True! We end up putting too much emphasis on some areas, too little on others. But balanced living is quite difficult to implement or maintain. Mainly because one aspect of life can suddenly become the most important and other things must take a backseat. Like when I am working on a big project, it can be 15–16-hour days, and my workout routine is often the first thing to get neglected."

"Maintaining balance is a constant battle because life exists between polarities. Work and rest. Darkness and light. Hills and valleys. You cannot escape them. All are needed. The existence of one lends meaning to the other. There are, obviously, exceptions. But if we don't convert exceptions into bad habits, we can achieve a balance over time. Having an insatiable drive is fine because it's often transferable to all aspects of life. The challenge is to avoid turning this drive into an obsession."

"Hmmm ... but the midpoint of balance is often shifting. Once you immerse yourself in the world, get busy with work, deadlines, people's opinions, world affairs, it's very difficult to maintain the same level of balance," he said.

"Then maybe look at balance as a quest for equilibrium, rather than the midpoint. The difference being that equilibrium is a state, whereas a midpoint is a place. If you make balance a part of your daily ritual. Like in my case, a daily practice of meditation helps me immensely in maintaining a sense of perspective and not leaning toward an extreme for long."

They had arrived at the last small town before a final ascent up the mountain was required to reach the village where Theo was stationed.

Nadia made a quick pit stop at a grocery store to pick up supplies for her camp. Steve took the opportunity to pick up a pack of Pringles and two bags of candy.

Nadia was still busy loading up the cart, so he strolled into a small bookstore next door.

As he was perusing the bestseller aisle, suddenly, he was struck by the idea of buying Nadia a gift, something that would remind her of their conversations. Who was he kidding—more like something that would remind her of him!

He asked the boy at the counter about the book by Kobe Bryant.

The store didn't have a computer at the front of the store, so the boy proceeded to the backroom to check if they had it in stock. As he waited, Steve browsed the tall wooden shelves next to the register, crammed with books on philosophy, religion, health, metaphysics. As he stepped back to look at the management section, he knocked over a pile of books stacked on a three-legged wooden stool.

Embarrassed, he swiftly bent over to pick them up when a familiar face flashed out of the back cover of a book lying on the floor. It was the Apricot Man!

He quickly picked it up and turned to the front cover. It had a stark white background, with a photo of a plate heaped with peaches placed alongside a steaming white cup of tea. The title read *The Productivity Paradox: Doing Less to Achieve More*.

He turned it over to the back cover, which included a brief profile of the author:

A successful venture capitalist, Edward Bernstein is an MBA from Stanford. After 30 years of successful leadership *stints at three technology companies in Silicon Valley, he moved to India to launch a venture capital firm with three Indian partners. Today, the company is one of India's leading venture capital firms, worth over $4.2 billion.*

No wonder he looked familiar when he first saw him.

He excitedly bought both books and came out of the shop to see Nadia waiting outside, flashing her phone.

"Hey, the mobile network seems to have been restored. So, you can call your boss now."

"That's great ... but look at this ... I just spent an amazing afternoon with this man yesterday," he said as he pointed to Bernstein's picture on the back cover.

"Oh, that's Eddie," she said.

"You know him? Do you also know this guy is funding some of the most interesting companies in AI technology today? And to think, I accused him of having no real-world experience. Gawd, I feel like a fool!" Steve laughed.

She smiled, offering him a packet of mixed trail nuts. "That's OK. I am sure if he wanted to tell you who he was, he would have."

"Actually, he avoided the topic entirely," Steve replied, scooping a handful of the mix. "But maybe it was all for the best. I was able to ask him a lot of questions I wouldn't have asked otherwise. I would have been too blinded by his accomplishments to pay any real attention to his answers."

"So does knowing about his background and book make you reflect differently about who he is?"

"Not really. He seemed like a very simple, purposeful man, devoid of any pretense," he said, chewing on a sweet date. "Considering he's a billionaire, there were no expensive gadgets at his cottage except for a good Bose music system and an expensive saxophone. Yet, his taste spoke of elegance. And whatever he did, he did as if it was the last thing he was going to do. I have never enjoyed a simple bowl of soup so much before," he said as he chucked a date pit far into the valley.

"Yes, joy can shine through the most ordinary experiences: a simple meal, a smile, a solution, a kind gesture, a thoughtful remark. But most of us are more interested in posturing. And the more success we obtain, the more compelled we feel to show it off ... bigger home ... bigger car ... latest gadgets. This clutter of possessions and displays only ends up making us anxious. Because the more we possess, the more bound we are to our possessions. And who *you* are frequently gets lost in all that noise."

"So true. It's because he surrounded himself with less that I noticed more of him. I paid more attention to what he was disclosing than what his belongings were presenting."

"Great. Then this trip is not turning out to be so bad," she asserted proudly, with a smile.

"Quite the opposite actually," he said, peering into her eyes and reciprocating the smile.

She stroked her hair self-consciously and bashfully turned away.

"Oh ... and that reminds me," he said promptly, "I must introduce your Eddie to Theo. Who knows, it might strike up a business opportunity?"

"Too late—they already know each other. They are chess partners."

"Grrrreat! There goes my pre-promotion pitch. Every time I plan to impress this guy, it backfires!"

Nadia laughed. "Then maybe you should stop trying so hard to impress him. Turn your efforts towards exciting your clients and inspiring your colleagues and team to achieve results collectively. What better way to impress the owner than that? And when it comes to the relationship with Theo, simply observe and listen this time. Instead of just seeing him as your chief, see him as a whole person you happen to know little about outside of projects at work. In Zen, it's called the Beginner's Mind, or seeing everything with a fresh pair of eyes."

"Hmm ... you have a point. I am so focused on saying the smart thing, the best thing, the cleverest thing, that I often miss fully engaging the person I am communicating with. I don't think I do it purposely; it's more out of habit. But, when I look back at my interactions, I often miss the moment, miss the truth the individual or group may be attempting to share or show me. And nothing has opened my eyes to this more than my journey here. And thank you for spelling that out. I needed that candidness. I do need to take in more than I blurt out."

"And don't forget to enjoy the moment! That's very important. Those moments often reveal the roadmap to your spark."

"I think I may already be making inroads in that department," he said, turning to face her. "I think I have a good idea of where I am going wrong."

"And that is?" she said.

"You mentioned polarities, and that got me thinking about passion and reason."

"Hmmm ... continue," she instructed, with a curious look.

"When I first graduated, I thoroughly enjoyed my work and had a strong motivation to give back as much as I took in. I was focused on finding as many opportunities as possible to give of myself and my skills to needy causes. In the same way, I was determined to perform well in my career pursuits. I felt quite in balance. But, somewhere along the way, the two-column approach shifted to a single pursuit. I saw everyone around me earning more, buying more, experiencing the best life could offer. And suddenly, I found myself pondering the mediocre life I came from. If I didn't focus on what everyone else around me was laser-focused on, would I survive in this dog-eat-dog world? Would I slowly find myself in the rear view of my colleagues, in mediocrity again? From that point, I think it all shifted. I was on a binge to own as many titles and as many things as I could. Things my parents could never dream of having. I never wanted to think twice about buying my dream car, purchasing the most expensive seats in the arena, dining at the best restaurants, obtaining memberships to the most exclusive clubs, and ... anyway, you get the point," he sighed.

"And ...?" She urged him on knowing full well this diatribe was much-needed therapy.

"I achieved ... every single one of those goals," he said.

"That must have made you very happy?" she asked, impressed.

"It did for a while. But it did not last. And now ..." He abruptly paused, turning to the heavens.

"Now?" she asked, after giving him a few moments to ponder.

"Now that I have achieved most of my goals, I realize I no longer have the same drive or reason to continue beyond this point. Of course, there are more promotions and bigger paychecks to aim for, but it's like I've already tasted enough of the power and riches. Hard to explain but ... it's like I have this first-class plane ticket but nowhere to go."

"Hmm," she nodded with slight concern.

"But I think it's not the work I need to change because I still enjoy the challenge. I just need to tweak my intentions for doing it. Shift my goalposts a little by instilling better rationale and good reasoning to my passions, so they don't feel so aimless and ... blind."

"I'm so happy to hear that, and I'm glad I could help," she said, bending down to tie her laces. He watched her as she worked on the knot, her elfin face with the button nose and wide eyes, her hair a tangled mess now, the simple T-shirt, the black cargos with their ends damp and muddy.

She was so different from the type of women he dated. It was both bizarre and exhilarating at the same time.

He loved listening to her when she spoke with wisdom beyond her years. To be fair, he also loved looking at her as she expressed herself. The way she squinted her eyes and crinkled the top of her nose, the dimples teasing her cheeks every time she smiled. The way she tilted her head when she pondered something. Her strong fingers as they gripped the mountainous rock as she climbed. The very same fingers, calm as they freed his shirt each time it became entangled in a bush, and yes ... how could he forget her voracious appetite for food ... for life!

"You more than helped. You gave me direction," he said quietly.

She glanced up at him, playfully frowning.

"I mean ... you ARE literally guiding me to my final destination—leading me to Theo," he explained honestly.

"You know what they say," she responded, sitting up, brushing the dried leaves off her trousers. "Everything happens for a reason. Even this meeting."

"I did not completely believe it before ... but now ... it's starting to make more sense. Maybe, there is a higher purpose at play."

"It's not a maybe. There's always a greater force in the mix. And the more you see, feel and acknowledge its presence, the more the whole universe appears connected," she said assuredly.

They had reached the foot of a giant deodar tree, where the path forked into two roads.

"And that connection seems so much clearer and more valuable when experienced with someone else," he said, smiling mischievously.

She stared at him questioningly before there was a flash of recognition in her eyes. She lowered her gaze, pretending to brush off some lint on her sleeve.

He smiled. He had not seen her flustered before. It gave him hope.

"Or maybe it just appears to be so," she said, nervously opening her knapsack and quickly closing it up again. "Only time can tell," she said, looking back at him, her gaze defiant.

"I'm OK with that!" he nodded with a straight face, unwilling to look away.

"And this is … where our paths diverge," she said, looking away at the mysterious, impenetrable, snow-capped peaks in the distance.

"Do they have to?" he asked, already knowing the answer.

She peered at him, pursing her lips, the ends slowly curling up into a smile. "For now, yes. Mine is over this mountain," she said, pointing to a soaring elevation on the left. "And yours is on this path and through those trees. Only three miles more to go. A mile ahead, you will reach a hanging bridge … now if …"

He interrupted her, handing her the book he had taken out from his bag, "This is for you."

"Oh, the book you mentioned! Thank you! I'll start on it tonight, by the fireside at the camp."

Steve stood there waiting, hesitating.

"Is there something else?" she asked.

"I hope there is," he answered.

"Excuse me?"

"Listen … I would like to meet you again. As many times as possible, before I leave." It rushed out of Steve's mouth before he had time to think about it. "For dinner, or whatever you choose," he added.

"I will let you know," she responded without hesitation.

"How?" he questioned, leaning towards her.

"Let me first figure out the 'why.' After that, the 'how' will be much easier," she replied, laying a hand on his shoulder and gently nudging him back as she turned towards the mountain.

Thinking about the woman who had just left him, Steve walked through the clearing in the trees, the pine needles crunching beneath his feet. A part of him couldn't help but laugh, surprised to see how a person he had only recently met now consumed so much of his mind. The other part admonished him for revealing his feelings so soon.

As he walked deeper into the woodlands, the forest orchestra came alive—the clamor of swallows, a robin calling out from its perch on an oak tree, a coon crying out high in the skies and a woodpecker clucking on the bark of silver fir. Closer to the ground, a band of crickets had strung up a ruckus around a mound of decaying leaves, while a large centipede, its scales catching the sun's glint, slithered surely but silently across Steve's path, bringing him to a halt.

He leaned against a huge fir and looked up to see the afternoon light sifting through the tall deodars, painting moving shadows on the ground. The spicy, woody scent of the rain-soaked earth rose in a cadence, soaking him with the memories of his grandmother's breezy mountain cabin in Alberta.

Trusting life? OK, he should try it. He had done all he could for now. Nadia knew how he felt. He had seen it in her eyes. If life did have a bigger plan for them together, it would find a way. He tried to shrug off his remaining worries and strode towards his destination.

Slowly, the trees thinned out and the mountain dipped down into a yellow-green meadow filled with dandelions shimmering in the humid haze. Steve hustled down the trail, relishing the warm afternoon sun and the clean, brisk air until he became aware of a different sound—rushing water. Suddenly, the air grew cool and moist.

Ahead of him, the meadow grew sparse, then abruptly ended in a sheer 200-foot drop. Steve glanced over the edge to a thick belt of river running through the cleft in the mountains. The river surged in brown, muddy fury over razor-sharp rocks.

There it was, just as Nadia had described. Theo's village was just across the gorge.

Steve squared his shoulders, painted his face with a confident smile, and stood ready for the most important meeting of his journey.

But where was the bridge? He remembered Nadia also mentioning he would need to cross one.

At first, he couldn't see anything. But then, a hundred feet to the left, behind a large leafless tree, he spotted it swaying in the wind. A flimsy contraption made of wooden boards tied with ropes, supported by two stout wooden poles at each end. The bridge dangled alone and precarious over the river.

He walked to the bridge, each step revealing a new detail less reassuring than the last. It was not a bridge—it was a death trap!

Holding on tight to the poles, he laid one probing foot on the plank. It groaned as the ropes tightened. The bridge bounced and jabbed at the air.

Steve willed himself not to look down. He dangled his other foot into the air as a pebble broke loose. For several seconds, it clattered and dashed against the sides of the gorge, followed by a soft plunk into the raging depths. Suddenly,

Steve was six years old all over again, being pushed off the diving board by the class bully. He remembered the interminable descent, his limbs flailing helplessly, culminating with a stinging slap of water across his back. He gulped back the bile rising in his throat. And, with every limb shaking, he groped his way back to the ledge.

He couldn't do it! And even if he tried, what was the guarantee the bridge would hold his weight? He could call Nadia and ask her for help. But he had grown up in a world where admitting weakness was more likely to inspire derision than compassion, and sobbing was likely to get you pushed further out of the way. Nevertheless, he was very close to crying anytime now.

To come so close and still be so far. And why hadn't Nadia warned him about the bridge, especially when he had revealed his fear of heights? She didn't care. But nothing mattered now. He was all alone, like always.

He was puttering about, trying to figure out what to do, when he heard a noise at the other end of the bridge. Light-headed from all the stress and anxiety; he couldn't make out the figure who stood there.

Steve rubbed his eyes. Now clear-eyed, he stared at a man dressed in a long white kurta and blue jeans, his hair ruffled, with a three-day beard on his face. Theo stared back.

For a moment, they peered at each other in amazement till Theo broke out in a large grin. "Steve … you made it!"

"Not quite …" Steve gulped, looking over at the bridge. "I'm afraid this bridge is not quite what I imagined it would be."

Theo smiled, "Don't worry. It may look flimsy, but it's sound. I had it checked with an engineer the first year I was here."

"But … I have acrophobia!" There, he blurted it out.

There was no other way.

"Understood. This bridge can bear the weight of only one person at a time. Otherwise, I would come to help you over. So, we have two options, Steve—you either go back and wait for the bus to drive you here, or you can attempt to cross the bridge. Whatever you choose is completely fine. But if you are willing to take a chance, I can guide you across from here."

To go back the entire way now seemed a waste of time. On the other hand, if he decided to cross the bridge, he could be flirting with death.

"Steve, it's like walking a tightrope. It may seem daunting, but once you master the basic technique, the rest of the steps will flow naturally."

Walking on a tightrope didn't sound too great to Steve, either. But he decided that since Theo lived here, he knew what he was talking about.

"OK, I'm all ears … tell me how to cross." Steve let out a big sigh, followed by a long gulp.

"Keep your spine straight and slowly lower your hips by bending your knees. That will bring your center of gravity closer to the bridge and help you find your balance."

Steve looked at the unsteady planks of the bridge as they swayed in the breeze.

"It's shaking a lot," Steve said fearfully.

"You can't do anything about the wind. But if you quiet your mind, bring it to a still, you will do your part to not add to the shaking. So, take your time and tell me when you feel ready."

Steve closed his eyes and took a long deep breath, summoning all his strength and his focus. He took his first tentative step, trembling convulsively in the very fiber of his being. The bridge jerked and bobbed below his feet. But then he took another step, willing himself to keep looking up, never down.

He took a few more agonizingly slow steps, and, surprisingly, the bridge's swaying slowed. Then, the wind stopped, and the bridge became steady. He quickly took a few more steps, hoping to keep the positive momentum going. This was not so bad, after all! He quickened his pace while the wind was still low, suddenly enthused by the idea of impressing Theo. Then, unexpectedly, the strap of his knapsack slipped down his shoulder and jerked the sack low, upsetting his balance. He tried to counter it by leaning forward, but the bridge started undulating wildly, nearly throwing him off.

"Slow down, Steve, slow down! And try not to lean forward or backward, or you will upset your balance."

He didn't have to be told to slow down. He was already frozen to the spot. And then, despite his best efforts, he looked down into the void. Sweat broke out from every pore, standing in big, cold beads on his forehead. He was too scared even to wipe his brow. He could die this very moment. All his big plans and ideas, extinguished in just one moment. And what was he leaving behind? What was his legacy? Nothing except for a few cars, a couple of homes, a bank balance and a handful of people who, related by blood, were obliged to mourn him. The poverty of his existence shamed him.

"Don't drift to one side or the other. Stay right in the middle and maintain a pace that works best for you."

Steve nodded, trying to quiet his mind. Somehow, the advice Theo was giving applied to both his position in life and this bridge. He could not give up ... not now ... not when he knew this was something he had to do. No more excuses.

Theo continued to galvanize his young staffer, "Keep your focus only on the next step. Nothing else exists right now. Remember, staying in balance will require you to work with your entire being—mental, physical, emotional and spiritual.

Your whole system needs to be in harmony. Collect yourself and take one step, then another and continue that sequence all the way here."

Steve exhaled through his mouth. As the wind slowed down again, he took a tiny, almost undetectable, step. But it was a step forward, nonetheless. He dragged his arms slowly over the cold, damp rope, with his eyes fixed on Theo's hand, which rested on a post on the other end. There was no looking right, left, ahead or behind. There was no other thought in his mind except for the next step. His entire existence encapsulated in this moment, he kept walking, and slowly, a rhythm emerged again.

Every time the wind picked up, he would pause and start again. But this time, his pauses were more measured, more purposeful. As he waited for the wind to subside, he slowly swung his head around to observe the view and, for the first time, savored the staggering beauty of the mountains and trees, as well as the brown, muddy river flowing down to the plains. His gaze fell on Theo, who still stood as still as a rock, his hands on the post, trying his best to avoid disturbing Steve's concentration.

When he finally reached the other side, Steve lunged at Theo, naturally locking him into an impromptu bear hug. They both laughed in relief. And Theo didn't hesitate for a moment to hug him back.

With no need for any more words, the duo silently made their way to the village.

The suburb consisted of a small cluster of simple mud and stone houses that dotted the mountain slope. Along the way, they passed shepherds leading a flock of sheep, farmers on their way to the fields, women scrubbing their courtyards, and children playing in a tiny clearing between trees. The air was a potpourri, filled with the smells of hay, cow droppings, wood smoke and the wild forest.

They walked until they arrived at a wooden gate. Behind it lay a long, newly constructed, two-story building. Behind it, a smaller building containing staff quarters peeked out. Theo unlocked the big house's front door and led Steve inside. Within, he saw a simple room with a cot, desk and wooden cupboard.

"Why don't you freshen up, and I'll organize some tea and snacks," Theo said. "You must be hungry after that climb."

An hour later, they were seated on the veranda, sipping tea and eating fried vegetable fritters. Steve had just handed the envelope to Theo, who had accepted it without preamble and put it away immediately without opening it.

They watched a group of young children in the garden who were engrossed in a painting lesson. The other classrooms were all filled with students in other sessions.

"Our company took over an abandoned half-finished government building and, after a bit of refurbishing, converted it into a school," Theo said after taking a sip of his tea. "The project was completed in collaboration with the local district administration. In the beginning, we didn't have any electricity, running water, phone lines or even an indoor toilet. But slowly and steadily, the building took shape. And today, we have over 150 children from the four surrounding villages studying here. The sad thing is, most of them are either living in poverty or live too far away to make it here, so many drop out midway. The severe poverty doesn't help, either, as it hinders the children's abilities to focus on their studies. But here, we take care of their entire education from the age of four to 16 and provide coaching to students who need more attention. We also have approximately 40 students who stay in our residential facilities."

"Where were these children studying before this was all built?" Steve asked, struck by the lack of infrastructure.

"Before all this, the only way to get an education was by traveling to a town across the river. Many of them had to use that bridge you so heroically traversed because they couldn't afford the bus fare."

"Oh, thank heavens you made this happen!" Steve said, his voice a mix of gratitude and shock. "I can't imagine children ever having to go over that horrible bridge."

"You're right; no child should have to go through all that to get an education. Now, we have a dedicated team working on building furniture for a new school wing. And we are planning the construction of an additional residential building in the adjoining field. With the new building, we'll be able to enroll another fifty children. However, land transfer approvals are delaying it."

"But how did you even come to know about this village? It's so remote."

"Nadia had contributed a piece to our India Newsletter, spotlighting how difficult it was for children in this region to receive even a basic education. Well, that got me thinking, and I decided to explore this whole area during my break to find out how we could make a difference."

"So, you know Nadia?" Steve said passionately.

"You thought I appeared at the bridge by magic?"

"Honestly ... after this trip, I am open to believing anything," Steve replied wryly, but he was secretly pleased that she had not deserted him.

Theo threw his head back, laughing.

"But seriously, I was surprised when Nadia told me you had decided to take the forest route instead of the bus, given your fear of heights."

"Ah well, it was partly overconfidence ... partly something else," Steve quipped.

Theo nodded, amused.

"How did you know about my fear of heights?"

"I remember, two years ago, at our company retreat, you refused to get on that zip line or try the bungee jump."

Steve was amazed that Theo not only remembered but even noticed in the first place.

"And when you arrived at that bridge today, you thought you were all alone?"

"Yes ... and when the bridge was swinging wildly, I thought for sure I wouldn't make it here to meet you. My second brush with death on this trip. It's funny how staring death in the face can immediately put everything into perspective."

"Like?" Theo probed.

"There were so many things that I thought about doing, accomplishing, but kept postponing. But now I know there is no later! It's time to stop living so blindly, thinking that I have infinite time just because I'm young, healthy and educated. This whole trip has been a warning bell—a lightning rod cautioning me to step up the pace on all the things I want to achieve, all the changes I want to make. And, as you've been talking, I've been thinking, I want to start with this school ..."

"But what about your meeting with Burton to close the deal?" Theo said politely.

"I'm not really worried about it anymore ... I've already done all I can for that deal. I think my contribution will be more valuable here. I've already emailed Susan to ask if she would be willing to meet with them in my place."

"Well then, that big bad bridge served you well," Theo smiled.

"Oh, not just that bridge! It feels like this entire trip has been a long, continuous bridge to the other side."

Steve collected his thoughts for a moment before speaking. "So, Theo, any chance we can meet the team making the school furniture? You don't know this about me, but in high school, I had to choose a vocational elective, and I happened to choose carpentry, never thinking it would be of any use for me … until now."

"Then why don't I introduce you to the building contractor," said Theo, rising from his seat. "He'll tell you exactly what's needed."

A week later, Steve was sawing. He was working alongside the carpentry team, building brand new benches using a blueprint he downloaded from the internet.

These were light, collapsible wooden desks that came with attached, solar-powered LED lamps. It would be easy for the children to carry them home for their nighttime studies even during power outages, which were frequent in the region.

Working day and night with the carpenters and artists, sprawled on the floor, surrounded by slabs of wood, chisels and hammers, Steve had time to reflect.

Even the most mundane wood polishing task felt like magic, a spark! He could finally take the time to observe the beautiful grain of the wood, the perfect symmetry of rings on a tree trunk. He also had time to enjoy the company of friends on warm sunny days and the many wood-stove-cooked meals he ate in the cool evening breeze. He had time to really hear the laughter of children and take in the unrelenting spirit of the earth in all its glory.

Every evening, the children swarmed around him, wide-eyed, paying rapt attention as he fashioned little wagon carts, spinning tops, and furniture for the dollhouses in the craft room from spare scraps of wood. The previous week, he had made a swing from a plank of wood and ropes strung around the branch of the peepal tree. Since then, he had become a hot favorite with the children. And now, the evenings were devoted to them. Strangely enough, he didn't seem to mind. In fact, he looked forward to it. With them, it was as if every commonplace thing further ignited the spark he was already nurturing in full force.

Every experience triggered a new thought—that he had been searching for his spark in all the wrong places. If he could find a spark in the simple art of chiseling a piece of wood, then the spark must not lie in the task itself; it must arise from within him. The spark always lived deep inside him. It only needed his acknowledgment and readiness to ignite.

Every day, he tried to follow his purpose—anything that spoke to the deepest part of him. Until he didn't have to look for the spark; it naturally burned in him.

Nothing in life would ever be mundane or jaded again if he was willing to do what was most important to him, to keep the spark kindled by living every moment fully.

Through his magnanimous quest, he had come to grips with the fact that destiny was not a fixed destination or even a given eventuality, for that matter. It was consistently changing and moving, being shaped by every intention he made, every action he took, every choice he made. Each choice, when imbued with humility, responsibility and a willingness to genuinely explore and do his best, could unleash a spirited spark.

And all this insight had been made possible because he now had the time to think. To look back and reflect on his life for long hours, without the constant interruption of a distracted life. His existence was no longer filled with inconsequential possessions, pursuits and activities that usurped the mental, emotional and spiritual space from where the spark could arise.

He wanted to share this newfound wisdom with Theo. He wanted to shout it out to the world! But he wanted to make sure that this feeling was real and not just a passing emotion before he revealed it to the world.

And there was still so much to be done—supplies to order, work schedules to organize, building plans to finalize, the district collector's approvals to forward to the Delhi office. So, Steve focused on planning the next ten days before the team took leave for Diwali celebrations.

The entire school had been festooned with strings of marigold flowers. The floor was painted in beautiful patterns made with colored rice flour. The aroma of clarified butter, fried almonds and thickened milk intermingled with the spicy, woody scents of the forest, creating a delightful essence that flowed freely in the air. And throughout the day, the villagers brought baskets of the freshest farm produce and scrumptious homemade sweets to help make the evening feast deliciously memorable.

After completing his chores, Steve rushed to his room to clean up.

A freshly-showered Steve came out of his room sporting a brand-new kurta—a gift from a fellow carpenter—when he saw them sitting on the stairs outside the veranda.

Raju, a sensitive eight-year-old boy who spoke little, and Sonal, his precocious five-year-old sister who couldn't stop jabbering, were an odd but highly complementary pair. Sonal was sitting there in a green frock, clutching her plastic doll to her chest and nibbling her stubby nails, while the boy looked at photos in an old copy of *National Geographic* that Steve had given him. Steve suddenly remembered he had promised to repair Sonal's doll. The arm had broken, and he had made her a promise to glue it back on.

He was about to call out to them when he saw Theo walking down the corridor towards his room, beaming.

"This was overdue … and I thought, what better occasion than Diwali to present it?" Theo said, handing him an envelope, which Steve recognized all too well.

Surprised, Steve accepted it and pulled out the sheaf of papers.

It was his promotion letter, announcing his promotion to the role of COO. He didn't believe it and had to read the letter one more time for it to sink in fully.

He threw his head back and laughed. "You mean … all this time, I had been carrying my promotion letter?!"

"Well, don't get too cocky. I hadn't signed it until a few minutes ago. It could have gone either way," Theo said, softly but sternly.

"And, all this time, I thought you didn't even like me," Steve grinned.

"You always struck me as capable, but I wanted to be absolutely sure of your fluency. You see, in leadership, there are two capabilities to management. One capability functions like the Machine, precise and unrelenting. The other, like the Being, is spontaneous and evolving. And I need someone who can operate in either role, depending on the situation. For that, the person needs to be open to learning *and* unlearning, questioning *and* answering, creating *and* absorbing new experiences, designing *and* exploring new possibilities. A team player who could look his biggest fear square in the eye and choose to never give up."

"Cultivating a beginner's mind," Steve added.

"Yes!" Theo replied, surprised. "And observing you in action, in person, was the only way to be sure you were ready for that type of challenge."

Steve stared intensely at the papers.

"Well, you seem awfully quiet for someone who has just been promoted," Theo noticed.

"I ... I don't know what to say," Steve replied, slowly making eye contact.

"Seriously? Wasn't this what you wanted? Or were you hoping for a bigger compensation package?" Theo asked.

Steve ran his hand through his hair, his mind strangely numb. He looked at the envelope with the papers now tucked back in it. There was no doubt that it contained everything he wanted. And the salary package was more than what he had been expecting. But why wasn't he excited? Why wasn't he going crazy with immense joy? What was wrong?

Steve took a moment to peer out the window. Sonal was now standing on her toes, waving her doll incessantly, while her brother kept pulling her back by her sleeve.

He could not help but laugh, a genuine chuckle with unbridled joy. And suddenly, it was all clear.

Turning back to Theo, he slowly but assuredly handed the envelope back. "Thank you, Theo ... thank you for this opportunity. Thank you for being you!"

"You don't need to thank me. You have been an asset to this firm, and I am looking forward to a great future for our company with you at the helm," Theo said, patting Steve on the back.

"Then give me a role where I will be at my best."

Theo glanced at the envelope, then back at Steve. "Isn't this what you asked for? Exactly what you wanted?"

"I did ... for a very long time. But now ..."

"Now ...?"

"Now, I feel different."

"I don't understand," Theo said, befuddled.

"I didn't either, for a very long time. Let me put it this way ... we all go through the ups and downs of life, good and bad days. But there are days which are plainly and simply spectacular! Stellar moments that define your life. Like the day I got accepted to Harvard. The day I won my first case. The day I bought my mother her own apartment. The day I got my dream job! But lately, I hadn't felt that spark. And for a long time, I kept blaming it on life. But it was not life. It was me. It was me who was not feeling it."

"Feeling what?" Theo probed, wanting to confirm what Steve was saying.

"My spark ... my raison d'être, my reason for Being, as you said. Until last week, the day I met with the land commissioner, when I was able to convince him to allocate the land for the new school. That was the day when I realized the spark was ignited again. And I could clearly see that everything I had accomplished so far had been driven by want, not a need, to escape the ignominy of a so-called mediocre existence. My ultimate dream was driven by a desire to be rich and successful, be someone who mattered in this world."

"Wait, are you saying you did not enjoy all that ... the hard work, the long nights, your accomplishments?"

"No, don't get me wrong. I enjoyed it all. In fact, I am grateful for every experience and achievement. And I am grateful to myself for striving for them. For if I hadn't lived that dream, I would have never arrived at this one. The last few years, I've had a lot of wins but also experienced a lot of turmoil. It's like I've been slowly walking further and further away from my happiness. But that day at the commissioner's office, I was finally using my skills for something I was truly passionate about. I felt alive! Excited! And strangely enough, I also felt a profound sense of peace. I felt like me again.

"There's something more to life than what we see, hear, touch. I still can't define it. All I can say is, I feel it now ... here," he said, pointing to his heart.

"So, what is the plan now?" Theo asked with great interest.

"So here is my proposal. And I think you will like it. Right now, our Corporate Social Responsibility projects are fragmented and sporadic. There's no better time to create a special division for all the CSR work we do across the world. And in a more open and welcoming format, where our colleagues and employees have the option to contribute their time and skills in a manner they like. I would be willing—honestly, more than happy—to reshape this division and advance our work with all our territorial offices. So, instead of promoting me to COO, I'm asking you for the VP of Corporate Social Responsibility position."

"Then who do you propose for the COO role?" Theo asked.

"I think it should be Susan. She is a perfect fit for the role."

"Be careful what you are asking for, Steve," cautioned Theo. "It's not easy to give up the life you've led so far. The big client meetings, the business lunches, the dinner parties, the excitement of a win … your killer instinct?"

Steve laughed. "Looks like you've been talking to your chess partner."

Theo shrugged. "Edward saw our company logo on the envelope when you bumped into him under that apricot tree."

"In that case, I'd like you to tell him I don't call my instinct 'killer' anymore."

"So, what do you call it now?"

"My spark. I've realized that as long as I am following what sparks my joy, my bliss—something that gives voice to my deepest values—the rest falls into place on its own. I no longer want to be led by ego, my fear of failure, but something far larger than myself."

"I'm impressed. But are you sure this is not a passing phase ... a reaction to the recent events in your life?"

"I agree; this knowing is recent. And yes ... the recent events have contributed immensely to my new outlook. And I completely understand that I will need to carefully tend to this knowing, integrate it in my actions so that it shifts from being an occasional experience to my way of life. It will require much more courage and commitment than what I displayed with my 'killer' attitude—a willingness to step out of my comfort zone. But I know that with the right people around me, it will be easier to achieve that state of mind."

Theo did not say a word but smiled.

"Well? What do you think about my idea? The CSR division?" Steve asked.

Theo extended his hand to Steve. "You're on! Meet me tomorrow at 9 a.m. sharp in my room. There are many plans we have to discuss."

"Great! We can even start now if you want," Steve said, overjoyed.

"No, I think right now you have more important people waiting ..." Theo chuckled, pointing at Sonal peeking into the window.

A big, lazy moon hung high in the autumn sky as Steve gobbled another laddu and helped Sonal light up a row of oil lamps lining the boundary wall. Now and then, the sky lit up in a shower of firework sparks as the entire town came together to celebrate the festival of lights.

And then, among the shining lamps, the sparkling sky and the garlands of marigold, he saw her. She pushed open the gate and walked up the lamp-lined path, the light bouncing off her hair, a glint of gold threading through her saree. She stopped and bent down to ask a child something, and Steve's heart stopped when the boy pointed in his direction.

Their eyes met. Nadia smiled. And at that moment, Steve saw with startling clarity the often invisible, hazy ways each event inspires, conspires and influences the trajectory of our lives. A course that leads us to the most subtle, yet most profound, part of us—our inner light, our soul. And sometimes, our soulmate, as well.

Because when we act from our inner light, every particle in the universe rises to fuel our SPARK!

Significance:
K for *Knowing*

> *"He who knows others is wise.*
> *He who knows himself is enlightened."*
>
> —Lao Tzu

In this chapter, Steve unexpectedly turned down the COO position, which he had been working towards his entire career. He does so because he intrinsically knows it's not only the right thing to do but the best move for him. This decision highlights how a deeper intuition comes from an inner Knowing, the K in SPARK.

Let's delve into how Knowing makes itself known in our lives:

Know the difference between Knowledge vs. Knowing.

Knowing is different from knowledge. It is internal. Knowledge can be acquired from reading, taking a class or practical lessons at work. It is external. Knowing, on the other hand, is a certainty that comes from experience, contemplation and reflection.

Knowledge is factual, while knowing is experiential. Knowledge has utility in this world. It makes you more efficient, skillful and resourceful, which may lead you to earn more. Knowing, meanwhile, is more elemental and innate. It's like the way a flower knows how to open, a fish knows how to swim, a child in the mother's womb knows how to grow, and you know how to breathe. This is a totally different kind of intrinsic intelligence. But unlike Knowledge, Knowing is not acquired; it is natural.

Osho, the Indian mystic, describes how one can go on thinking and accumulating information, but also how pieces of information are nothing more than "paper boats" that will not help in an ocean voyage. If you remain on the shore and only discuss your voyage in theory, these paper boats seem like real boats. But if you go on the voyage with paper boats, you will indeed drown. Only when you transcend the mind do you become "original." However, to be "original" and present, you need to stop clinging to Knowledge. Life's outlook is transformed when you cooperate with the forces of life rather than oppose them. Knowing is about trusting life and accepting our existence, as is, now!

As we know, Steve surprisingly declined the job offer to become COO and instead chose the path of becoming VP of CSR. He was able to shift gears like this because he was fortunate enough to have that option. However, you may not necessarily have that leeway or even the desire to change your job title or career. In that case, there are many other ways to recalibrate an existing job to allow room for more fulfilling aspects in your life. Never hesitate to explore those channels, especially if you have a deeper Knowing that it is the right thing to do.

Cultivate the beginner's mind.

As counterintuitive as it may sound, the first stage of Knowing is not knowing. Not knowing has a beauty of its own, a purity. By cultivating the beginner's mind and being willing to "not know," you allow the possibilities for Knowing to emerge.

So, what is the beginner's mind? The beginner's mind is an element of Zen practice that is motivated by an unbound awareness. It is the mind that is innocent of preconceptions, expectations, judgments and prejudices. A popular Zen Buddhism story tells us about an emperor, also a devout Buddhist, who invites a great Zen master to his palace to ask him deeper questions about Buddhism.

"What is the highest truth of the holy Buddhist doctrine?" the emperor asked.

"Vast emptiness … and not a trace of holiness," the master replied.

"If there is no holiness," the emperor said, "then who or what are you?"

"I do not know," the master replied.

Therefore, not knowing is not ignorance; not knowing is a state of innocence. There is neither knowledge nor ignorance; both have been transcended. The mind can be knowledgeable, and the mind can be ignorant. Not knowing simply means a state of "no mind." Knowledge and ignorance are only different in terms of the quantity of information, not in their qualities. However, tapping into a deep-seated Knowing transcends both knowledge and ignorance.

Be present through meditation and mindful observation.

Meditation and mindful observation are about paying attention to an experience in the present moment in an accepting, non-judgmental way. Mindful observation heightens your ability to evaluate your actions and behaviors in relation to your goals. Mindfully observing your actions and behaviors opens you up to the realization that they are usually not what you think they are. This type of widened observation helps you become focused on what is most important to you. Attentive observation heightens your awareness and shifts your behavior to squarely focus on your goal.

The benefits of meditation are well documented and include better problem-solving, brain synchronization, enhanced memory, better sleep and an enhanced capacity for focus and attention.

To thrive, we need to involve more than our thinking mind. Research shows that it is not thinking but felt experience that opens doors to new ways of being. Before beginning an activity, engage your breath and pay attention to what is happening in the present moment. This will allow you to have total focus on the task at hand. The moment you feel this intensity of focus, you are entering the realm of mindfulness.

Live in "day-tight compartments."

In his wonderful book *How to Stop Worrying and Start Living*, Dale Carnegie shares a simple but great metaphor of living life in "day-tight compartments." Day-tight compartments, a term first coined by Sir William Osler, call for people to stay fully focused on the moment, on today. To be in control of only what is within the present "compartment," not in the compartments behind you, far ahead of you, or even to the side of you. By shifting your attention from the past, future and any irrelevant concerns—all of which are out of your control—you will have more capacity to invest in the present moment.

There is nothing else except the present moment. The present moment is where all the meaning lies and where all future possibility rests. The Sufis say, "To grasp the present moment is to grasp eternity itself." They believe that "you can plan for 100 years, but you don't know what will happen the next second." Life is indeed uncertain and unexpected, but we are the masters of this moment. To be living and healthy today is a priceless gift to savor, cherish and celebrate. Use this gift to make each day count. Live this moment intensely, passionately and fully, for it will meet you but once. Make it the primary focus of your life. Plunge daringly into it.

Strive for a balanced life.

Inner Knowing requires a sense of balance and harmony. It's about doing less to achieve more. It also means finding happiness in small things. Staying in balance requires you to understand your whole being. You must know your physical, mental and spiritual needs, and you must bring them into congruence. If you do not understand how each contributes to your whole, you may end up catering to one facet of your life at the expense of the whole. If you can understand your whole in relation to its parts, you can determine the amount of time and effort you will need to invest in each facet.

Taoists represent this as a balance between Yin and Yang. This principle symbolizes the balance of opposites in the universe. When Yin and Yang are in balance, all becomes calm. When and if one outweighs the other, confusion and disarray are likely to set in.

Balance is the happy medium between the minimum and the maximum; it is the optimum. The minimum represents the least you can do to get by, while the maximum is the most you are capable of. The optimum, therefore, is the amount or degree of anything that creates a minimum-maximum life harmony.

Respect your intuition and act on gut feelings.

One day I inadvertently came across a heart-warming story about a man foregoing a meeting with the president at the White House. He made a heart-centered choice to attend his son's championship basketball game instead. This choice stemmed from an intuition or gut feeling, though his head may have been saying something different. Well, it so happened that he was wise to listen to his gut. His son, after a long-fought tight game, eventually hit the all-important, buzzer-beating winning shot and secured the trophy. He later said that the experience of watching his son make the winning shot was worth far more than going to the White House to meet with the president.

After reading this story, I too was inspired. I dropped everything I was doing to go watch my son play his soccer game. I did so even though I knew I could only watch the first five minutes of the match, as I had to pick my wife up from work soon after. I arrived at the soccer pitch just in time as the game was about to start. As I often do, I called out to my son, "I'm here!" He gave me the thumbs up. Then, I reminded him that I could only watch the game for five minutes. He again gave me the thumbs up. I just could not resist, so I said to him with a smile that if he was planning to score a goal, he had better do so in the next five minutes. He again gave me the thumbs up.

Astonishingly, right before the five-minute mark, he found the net! From about 25 yards out, he slipped the ball between two players and tucked it in the bottom right corner. Could a simple prompt from me have given him subconscious ammunition to set a goal to score in the first five minutes and follow through? I'd like to believe so. Although I normally would not have mustered the energy to go across town from my wife's office to watch just a few minutes of his game, this experience illustrates that spending even five minutes of quality time with someone you love can be transformative.

Place the utmost importance on your SPARK!

We often see success as being all about the big things, big jobs, big houses, big cars and big bank accounts. But real happiness often lives within the small things. Having loving relationships, enjoying quality time with family and living a principled and balanced life are all you need to be truly happy. At the end of the day, we are social beings—village dwellers—who require authentic connections that are implanted in non-material requirements. No number of possessions can buy this. And if they do, it's temporary.

The decision one makes around one's calling in life, as Steve does when offered the COO job, is not as easy as an impromptu decision to watch your son's game for five minutes. This requires a Knowing—a certainty!

This state of congruent confidence comes from a SPARK that embodies the importance of Service, Purpose, Attraction, Resilience and Knowing.

REFLECTION QUESTIONS:

- In what areas of your life could you prioritize Knowing over knowledge?

- How can you cultivate a beginner's mind rather than trying to amass knowledge? Do you have any role models who practice these principles that you could learn from?

- Are you fully tuned in to the present moment? If not, what is holding you back? What do you spend most of your time thinking about?

- What is your approach to juggling different facets of your life? How do you balance your life between spirituality, family, health, work, finance and lifelong learning?

HOW TO GET STARTED:

- Start making the time today onwards to mindfully observe life deeply. Spend time in nature and focus on the details of all the miracles occurring in this moment. Write down some ideas about how you could do this today.

_____
_____
_____

- Practice meditation 20 minutes a day, three to four times a week. Try using a service such as Calm or Headspace on your smartphone to guide you if you have never tried meditating before. Write down some ideas about when you could add meditation into your schedule or what apps or techniques you'd like to use.

_____
_____
_____

- Write a list of the most important aspects of your life and try to assess which ones need prioritization or reprioritizing.

_____
_____
_____

- Think about the aspects of your life that give you energy, happiness and meaning. Then, think about how much time you are spending on these areas.

　　_____
　　_____
　　_____
　　_____

- Live fully just for today (day-tight compartment) and focus on being the best version of yourself in this moment. Write down some ideas about how you can start doing this today.

　　_____
　　_____
　　_____
　　_____

Final Thoughts

I hope this book has been both enjoyable and enlightening for you. Now that you have read Steve's story and discovered the SPARK principles, I'd like to share my personal journey with you, which in some ways resembles our protagonist's pilgrimage to discovering his calling.

My own 'Journey from Success to Significance' began in 1997, when I stumbled upon an incredible opportunity for *Service.* Based on my financial planning experience as an accountant, I was asked to volunteer at an Afghan refugee camp in Pakistan. I went to Pakistan on a voluntary assignment to find out the financial needs of the Afghan refugees. My accounting degrees qualified me for such an assignment, but they did not prepare me for what lay ahead.

I took a taxi from my hotel to a refugee camp. At the camp, I was escorted to a tent that was a home for 14 refugees. A 14-year-old girl shared, "We walked for days through the mountains to escape the war. My cousin gave birth to a baby, and my mother fell sick, but we had to keep walking to survive." The mom in her late thirties shared: "My sister saw her husband being brutally murdered." It was heartbreaking to hear these stories. A 16-year-old boy told me: "In Pakistan, we needed to earn money to supplement some aid we were getting. So, we sold corn in a market for 14 hours a day and made about $1." It seemed that they were clinging to life with nothing but each other.

Outside the tent were many women and children. I was dressed in a suit and tie so they thought I was an important person who could help them. I stood there for no more than 60 seconds, but it seemed like forever. They stared at me with hope in their eyes. I did not know what to do. So, like a coward, I walked back to my taxi. In the 25-minute taxi ride back to my hotel, I shivered and sweated simultaneously. I sobbed like a baby. My soul was shaken.

In my air-conditioned hotel room, I curled up into a ball on the king-size bed. I cried for what seemed like hours. I saw images of the refugee children with their rosy cheeks, big eyes and smiles on their faces despite their plight. I played out, repeatedly, the scenes of horror. I went back and forth from emotions of hopelessness, to a renewed zest, to finding solutions. Not just as a volunteer interviewer but by espousing something greater.

I fell asleep. When I awoke, my mind's eye saw a fork in the road ahead. If I went left, I could continue living my comfortable lifestyle and ignore the powerful experience I had at the camp. The road to the right would take me on a quite different journey filled with obstacles as I tried to play my part in creating a positive impact. I struggled with this dilemma but knew deep down that there was no turning back. What would you do? I am sure you too would want your life to matter. It took me only a few seconds to decide; such was the might of that experience. I was inspired, hopeful and driven. I felt that I had found a cause that I would die for—a feeling that I had not experienced in the 43 years of my life. This was a pivotal moment for me. The irony was that by finding a cause that I would die for, my new life began! It reminded me of the Mark Twain quote I used earlier in the book: "There are two important days in your life. The day you are born, and the day you find out why." For me, it was like I found out the second important day—finding out why I was born. I had found my *Purpose.*

For the rest of my time in Pakistan, my head exploded with possibilities. My inner voice kept pointing me in the direction of speaking and writing about the power of giving. My purpose changed from "accounting for business" to "accounting for life." I was willing to "jump off the cliff backward" by foregoing three professional degrees, two businesses and a lavish salary to promote my Live to Give message. With this message, I could create an impact and change lives! Most people spend a lifetime looking for their purpose. Some die never finding it. I found my purpose and my spark in one visit to a refugee tent! A priceless gift!

Discussing my career change from accounting to speaking and writing with my wife Farzana brought me back to reality. She said: "Our daughter Sahar is eight and son Tawfiq three. How do you plan to pay for their university costs?" I bet you would have said the same things if you were in her shoes! My energy and enthusiasm zapped!

After a lot of back-and-forth, she eventually came around with one strong condition—that we don't sell our accounting businesses. Luckily, I listened to her as the first decade of my journey was full of challenges and obstacles. With the support of my wife Farzana and my business partner Kend, I was able to sustain my journey despite enormous obstacles. This was their way of practicing the Power of Giving.

I experienced enormous roadblocks at the beginning of my new career, including speaking several hundred times around the world and spending several thousand hours writing my first book before I could even cover my own expenses. Throughout the many years of struggle during my journey, I had the opportunity to practice my **Resilience**.

After discussing this career change with my wife, I began withdrawing from the two accounting firms we owned by empowering my partners and team. In 1998 I spoke more than 150 times around the world and did not make any income. In 1999 I had more than 170 speaking engagements around the world and published my first book, *Seven Steps to Lasting Happiness*, which still barely covered my expenses.

Then, in 2000, I went through a dark moment in my new career. Just before leaving for the UK to give a series of keynote speeches on lifelong learning, I stopped by a Vancouver bookstore to see whether my self-published book had arrived. I awkwardly searched for my own book on the store's computer. The computer showed no results. Then, I shyly typed in "Azim Jamal" and was confronted by a disheartening message: "Author Unknown." That was one of my lowest points; I had put all my money and thousands of hours of my time into this business, and I couldn't even get a book into the bookstore. I had let down my wife and children. I had given up a successful, lucrative career to follow a pipe dream. I felt I had made a mistake.

Filled with self-doubt, I was about to leave the store when I spotted a book titled *The Greatest Salesman in the World* by Og Mandino. I almost walked out anyway, but I was drawn to the book by some magnetic connection. I picked it up and, flipping to the introduction, I read how Mandino had been on the verge of suicide after he went broke, and his wife and child had walked out on him. Despite this, he managed to turn his life around when a visit to the public library saved his life and turned him into an aspiring author. Through positive thinking and determination, he went on to sell more than 30 million books. I was inspired! To me, that was a message from the Universe telling me that if Og could do it, I could do it too. When I was at my wits' end, the inspiration I needed was delivered to me.

Over the years, I continued to persist until I succeeded. The *signs* that I received along the way helped me realize that I was doing the right thing. My clear vision had led to many "accidents" that demonstrated how the Universe was positively conspiring to provide me opportunities to achieve the success that I desired. It continuously infused the magnetic energy I needed to attract results through **Attraction.** While I faced many roadblocks along my way to success, I also noticed several coincidences and divine encounters that solidified my belief that "what you seek is seeking you."

Just after the Afghan war in 2001, I traveled with a group of volunteers to Kabul, Afghanistan, via helicopter. Two helicopters—one carrying soldiers, the other carrying volunteers like me—flew in tandem into the city. In a disastrous circumstance, the aircraft carrying the soldiers crashed and everyone aboard perished. We, as volunteers, were incredibly fortunate to have survived. After this near-death experience, I was shaken! My heart broke even more when I witnessed orphans who had lost their parents in the war begging on the streets. At a low point, I walked past a rug shop where, amongst a plethora of intricately crafted rugs, I saw a tapestry that read, "Obstacles are what you see when you take your eye off your goal." I saw this as another Universal sign that was telling me I needed to continue to find inspiration and optimism, even in these sad circumstances. This became a mantra that I carried throughout the rest of my life.

When my first book, *Seven Steps to Lasting Happiness,* came out in July 1999, I was advised to send it to Robin Sharma, the author of *The Monk Who Sold His Ferrari,* among other books. I did so right away. Robin replied that he had seen my book at a bookstore in Toronto just a couple of days previously and that he liked what he saw. That exchange led to Robin becoming a dear friend and great mentor to me for the past two decades!

Some years later, I met Deepak Chopra, who was then the President of the Alliance for New Humanity. I was invited to speak at a conference for the Alliance in Puerto Rico. Deepak and I were both driven from the airport in the same vehicle. I found him genuine and down-to-earth, and we had a good chat on the way. At the event the next day, I had the honor of speaking on the same stage as Deepak. When Deepak later came to Vancouver, I met him at a small group gathering where I gave him my book, *Seven Steps to Lasting Happiness*. I had not asked for any endorsements or feedback, but two weeks later, I got a letter from the Chopra Center. I opened it only to find that the letter was addressed to someone else! I sent the letter back to them and asked if there was something else that was supposed to be sent to me. There was no reply. So I wrote to Deepak directly, referred to his great speech, asked if he had a chance to read my book and if he liked it and would be open to endorsing it. Lo and behold, he sent back a great endorsement! If I had not received the letter from the Chopra Center by mistake, I am not sure if I would have ever asked for an endorsement at all.

Several years later, Dr. Wayne Dyer was scheduled to speak in Vancouver about his then-new book, *The Power of Intention*, to a sold-out crowd. I found out about this too late, so I had to phone one of the organizers to ask if I could purchase a ticket. To my surprise, she said, "Azim, you would be a perfect choice to introduce him, and we would be delighted to have you as our guest." So, I had the opportunity to introduce Dr. Wayne Dyer at this sold-out event and demonstrate how the *Power of Intention* was truly at play. After my introduction, Dr. Dyer hugged me on the stage and told the crowd that this was the best introduction he had ever received! After his speech, I got to spend some time with him in the lounge, where he reiterated his feelings about my introduction. He later wrote a powerful quote for my book, *The Power of Giving*. Because I had the intention to hear him speak, not only did I get a chance to do that—I also attracted an opportunity to speak at his event, meet him and get a wonderful book endorsement!

The first time I met Jack Canfield in LA, I asked him the secret behind the phenomenal success of the *Chicken Soup for the Soul* series. He said that he and his co-author, Mark Victor Hansen, had hundreds of ideas to promote their books but decided that they would only do five things daily. By consistently doing five things daily, they sold over 100 million copies! Jack Canfield later wrote a foreword for *The Power of Giving*. In his international bestseller, *The Success Principles,* he kindly shares a paragraph about my work!

Most recently, I have had the privilege to do several live events with Brian Tracy in a few countries. We also have done several TV and radio interviews together. He was one of my favorite authors and speakers when I was growing up.

I have now authored nine books, including *Life Balance the Sufi Way* with Dr. Nido Quebin and *What You Seek is Seeking You* with Brian Tracy. In addition, Ken Blanchard, Bob Proctor, Seth Godin, Dr. John Demartini, Marshall Goldsmith, Harvey Mackay, Dr. Wayne Dyer, Deepak Chopra, Jack Canfield, Robin Sharma, Brian Tracy, Roger and Rebecca Merrill (Stephen Covey's co-authors)—some of the absolute best in the industry—have all endorsed my work. These were some of my favorite authors and speakers, and I aspired to be like them. These encounters were no coincidences. Because my aspirations were larger than self, I attracted some of the top inspirational speakers and leadership coaches into my life! However, the big question remains: have I realized my dream?

In answering this deeper question, I have had the opportunity to develop an inner **Knowing** to guide my spiritual and physical journey in this world.

From one perspective, the answer is: absolutely not! We never quite arrive because every time we reach our destination, we find that our destination has changed. Throughout our lives, we continue to aspire to reach new goals.

From another perspective, the answer is a resounding yes! Firstly, I took on every speaking engagement I could get to inspire audiences to give more of their time, knowledge and money. I spoke to over a million people in 100 cities across five continents and encouraged them to give more. Speaking at one charity event, we raised a million dollars in one evening!

My second approach was to write and inspire people to give more. I co-authored the book *The Power of Giving* with fund-raiser Harvey McKinnon. The book won the Nautilus Gold Award for books that change lives, was translated into ten languages and reached #1 on Barnes and Noble and Amazon (above *Harry Potter*!). The copyright of the book, as well as 100% of the revenues, are donated to a charitable organization. My latest book, *SPARK,* shows people how to go from Success to Significance by practicing the Live to Give message.

My third approach was to volunteer on projects within the Ismaili Muslim Community, which I am part of. I have been averaging 20-25 hours a week for the past 20 years. We took the approach of helping people like the ones I met at the refugee camp to become the masters of their destiny.

I have the full support of my wife Farzana, the respect of both my children Sahar and Tawfiq and had the blessings of my parents when they were still alive. My daughter has followed in my footsteps by giving up her successful career at large companies like Johnson & Johnson to start a maternal and child health social enterprise in Kenya. I am making a positive difference every day, and I have been blessed with SPARK.

To the best of my ability, I practice living fully in day-tight compartments, aligned with a compelling vision, maintaining life balance by regularly spending quality time with family and continually investing in lifelong learning, health, finance, spirituality, voluntary service and work. My goal has always been to walk my talk, and if I remain faithful to this pursuit no matter what, my voluntary service, inspirational speaking, leadership coaching and writing will continue to ring true.

Through service, purpose, attraction, resilience and knowing, I continue to strive …

However, a lot more needs to be done. According to the UN, we still have more than 700 million people living in extreme poverty around the world. Imagine more than the entire population of the USA, Canada, Australia, New Zealand, and the Middle East going to bed hungry at night!

Therefore, my plea to you is to begin or enhance your giving to attract your SPARK.

How would you like to: Have a spring in your step, A glow in your being, and Flow with oomph—no matter what?

Your SPARK is not dependent on outside factors such as pandemics or the economy. It is based on what is inside you.

Come SPARK the world alight with me!

End Notes

Swain, James E., Sara Konrath, Stephanie L. Brown, Eric D. Finegood, Leyla B. Akce, Carolyn J. Dayton, and S. Shaun Ho. "Parenting and beyond: Common Neurocircuits Underlying Parental and Altruistic Caregiving." Parenting 12, no. 2-3 (2012): 115–23. https://doi.org/10.1080/15295192.2012.680409.

Santi, Jenny. "The Science behind the Power of Giving (Op-Ed)." LiveScience. Purch, December 1, 2015. https://www.livescience.com/52936-need-to-give-boosted-by-brain-science-and-evolution.html.

Suttie, Jill Suttie Jill, and Jason Marsh Jason Marsh is the editor in chief of Greater Good. "5 Ways Giving Is Good for You." Greater Good, n.d. https://greatergood.berkeley.edu/article/item/5_ways_giving_is_good_for_you.

Mogilner, Cassie, Zoë Chance, and Michael I. Norton. "Giving Time Gives You Time." Psychological Science 23, no. 10 (2012): 1233–38. https://doi.org/10.1177/0956797612442551.

"The Science of Generosity - Phase II." John Templeton Foundation, n.d. https://www.templeton.org/es/discoveries/the-science-of-generosity.

Aknin, Lara B., J. Kiley Hamlin, and Elizabeth W. Dunn. "Giving Leads to Happiness in Young Children." PLoS ONE 7, no. 6 (2012). https://doi.org/10.1371/journal.pone.0039211.

Aknin, Lara B., Christopher P. Barrington-Leigh, Elizabeth W. Dunn, John F. Helliwell, Justine Burns, Robert Biswas-Diener, Imelda Kemeza, Paul Nyende, Claire E. Ashton-James, and Michael I. Norton. "Prosocial Spending and Well-Being: Cross-Cultural Evidence for a Psychological Universal." Journal of Personality and Social Psychology 104, no. 4 (2013): 635–52. https://doi.org/10.1037/a0031578.

"A Purpose-Driven Life May Last Longer." Harvard Health, September 1, 2019. https://www.health.harvard.edu/mind-and-mood/a-purpose-driven-life-may-last-longer.

Wolters Kluwer Health: Lippincott Williams and Wilkins. "Sense of purpose in life linked to lower mortality and cardiovascular risk." ScienceDaily. www.sciencedaily.com/releases/2015/12/151203112844.htm.

Sinek, Simon. Simon Sinek, n.d. https://simonsinek.com/.

https://langleygroupinstitute.com/wp-content/uploads/Interview-with-MC.pdf

"What Is a Flow State and What Are Its Benefits?" Headspace, n.d. https://www.headspace.com/articles/flow-state.

Burchell, Helen. "Capt Sir Tom Moore: How the Retired Army Officer Became a Nation's Hero." BBC News. BBC, February 2, 2021. https://www.bbc.com/news/uk-england-beds-bucks-herts-52324058.

Simpson, Mona. "A Sister's Eulogy for Steve Jobs." The New York Times. The New York Times, October 30, 2011. https://www.nytimes.com/2011/10/30/opinion/mona-simpsons-eulogy-for-steve-jobs.html.

Shin, Jihae, and Katherine L. Milkman. "How Backup Plans Can Harm Goal Pursuit: The Unexpected Downside of Being Prepared for Failure." Organizational Behavior and Human Decision Processes 135 (2016): 1–9. https://doi.org/10.1016/j.obhdp.2016.04.003.

Chowdhury, Madhuleena Roy. "The Neuroscience of Gratitude and How It Affects Anxiety & Grief." PositivePsychology.com, January 7, 2022. https://positivepsychology.com/neuroscience-of-gratitude/.

Introducing...
AZIM JAMAL, Inspirational Speaker and Leadership Coach

Azim Jamal is the founder of Corporate Sufi Worldwide Inc., a company dedicated to inspiring and empowering leaders to achieve material success, blended with a deep sense of purpose, passion and fulfillment. He calls this the synergy of Business, Balance & Beyond, and it's achieved by unleashing the power within that we all share.

Azim is the author of several highly-acclaimed books, including *What You Seek Is Seeking You*, co-authored with Brian Tracy. He has twice been a #1 Amazon bestselling author. He has also been a #1 bestseller with Barnes & Noble with his co-authored book *The Power of Giving*, which won the Nautilus Gold Award in May 2009 for books that create social change. Azim's books have been translated into ten languages.

Most importantly, Azim is a living, breathing example of the Corporate Sufi message. His dynamic, inspiring and thought-provoking message has been heard live by over 1 million people in more than 100 cities on five continents. And his media message has reached more than 5 million people around the world.

For more information on Azim and the Corporate Sufi philosophy

Visit:
www.corporatesufi.com

Stay connected:
blog.corporatesufi.com

Follow me on:
Twitter - twitter.com/Corporate_Sufi (@Corporate_Sufi)
Youtube - Azim Jamal
Facebook - @CorporateSufiOfficialPage
Linkedin - Azim Jamal

Praise for Azim's Work

His thought leadership, combined with his passion, energy and authenticity, have earned rave reviews from top CEOs, entrepreneurs, senior executives and startups, all of whom learned the secret to unlocking and unleashing their leadership greatness in the Corporate Sufi way.

"I have spoken alongside Azim Jamal several times and found his presentations authentic, congruent and highly effective. He speaks from the heart, so no wonder his message enters other people's hearts. Highly recommend him!"

Brian Tracy, one of the finest
inspirational speakers of all time

YPO ENDORSEMENTS

Young President Organization (YPO) is the global platform for chief executives to engage, learn and grow. Altogether, YPO member-run companies generate US$ 6 trillion in annual revenues and employ 15 million people.

"*Very relevant! I found the message of living a life of purpose refreshing and plan to practice some of his inspiring and practical messages.*"

Shesh Kulkarni, YPO, Bangalore

"*Azim puts profound things in a humble, unassuming manner—remarkably poised! I am going to work on taking a more holistic approach going forward. Thank you.*"

Gaurav Jalan, YPO, Calcutta

"*Azim helped me negotiate credit terms with a valued customer that resulted in net 15 days receivables on a 6 million US dollar contract that spanned over 8 months.*

Azim has also extended his help and seminars to our top personnel and key partners. If you are considering working with Azim, know that you will get a smart, humble, fantastic human being that will have your best interests at heart."

Fernando Sumaza, YPO, Puerto Rico

EO ENDORSEMENTS

The Entrepreneurs' Organization (EO) is a global business network of 12,000+ leading entrepreneurs in 167 chapters and 52 countries.

"Azim Jamal's message about Business, Balance & Beyond to the EO group at the Four Seasons Hotel in Mumbai was absolutely 5 star! I highly recommend his message."

Niraj Ambani, Reliance Industries
EO, India

"I rate Azim Jamal's message about Business, Balance & Beyond to the EO Group 10 out of 10! His insights into time and self-management are excellent."

Salil Chaturvedi MD, Provogue India Limited
EO, India

"Thank you for the fantastic presentation that you put on for our staff. Based on the feedback that I received from managers and employees alike, you really touched them. They took to heart the many excellent recommendations that you made and I have already seen positive changes as a result of your presentation."

Hanif Muljiani, EO, Vancouver

CORPORATE RECOGNITION & ADVOCACY

"I would highly endorse your presentation on 'Time Management.' The feedback received from ALL participants was overwhelmingly positive. Your message gave the audience a renewed sense of passion and motivation."

> Harpreet Singh, Senior Manager, Centurion Bank (now merged with HDFC Bank) Conference, India

"Azim was able to strike the right chord that most of us in the corporate world are facing on a daily basis."

> Amar Variawa, GM, Corporate Affairs, John Deere India Private Limited

MEDIA & PERSONALITY REVIEWS

"Life altering experience..."

> Times of India

TEDx TALK: LIVE TO GIVE

Azim explains how instilling a simple habit of purposeful daily giving can reward you with a more fulfilling life. Search YouTube for "Azim Jamal Live to Give"

Develop Your SPARK and Transform Your Success to Significance

If you have read the book and have been inspired to infuse a change in your personal and professional life, we are ready to help.

To boost your efforts in applying the SPARK principles and to help shift your focus from Success to Significance, Azim has created a highly-effective and interactive seven-week online program that is guaranteed to recharge your mindset, sharpen your skills, and inspire action. To join the SPARK: Journey from Success to Significance movement, please visit www.corporatesufi.com or email info@corporatesufi.com for all the details.

Stay connected:
blog.corporatesufi.com

Follow me on:
Twitter - twitter.com/Corporate_Sufi (@Corporate_Sufi)
Youtube - Azim Jamal
Facebook - @CorporateSufiOfficialPage
Linkedin - Azim Jamal

Manufactured by Amazon.ca
Acheson, AB

16640053R00127